FREE SPEECH ON CAMPUS

FREE SPEECH ON CAMPUS

ERWIN CHEMERINSKY

HOWARD GILLMAN

With a New Preface

Yale

UNIVERSITY PRESS

New Haven and London

Yale University Press books may be purchased in quantity for educational, business, or promotional use. For information, please e-mail sales.press@yale.edu (U.S. office) or sales@yaleup.co.uk (U.K. office).

Set in Janson Roman and Monotype Van Dijck types by
IDS Infotech, Ltd.
Printed in the United States of America.

Library of Congress Control Number: 2017934372
ISBN 978-0-300-22656-0 (hardcover : alk. paper)
ISBN 978-0-300-24001-6 (pbk.)

A catalogue record for this book is available from the British Library.

10 9 8 7 6 5 4 3 2 1

For our students

Contents

Preface to the Paperback Edition

In the years before we finished this book (in December 2016), debates about free speech on campuses had occasionally become heated. But even the most intense controversies were tame compared to what happened in early 2017, when alt-right provocateur Milo Yiannopoulos was scheduled to speak at UC Berkeley.

Despite vigorous student protests, the university had taken steps to ensure that the event would take place. Other University of California campuses sent police reinforcements, a wide perimeter was established around the venue, and barricades were set up to create a safety zone between protestors and people attending the event.

But then Berkeley faced something that other campuses had not experienced: 150 black-clad rioters associated with the anarchist group "Black Bloc"—many of them wearing masks, helmets, and body armor, and armed with poles, sticks, and commercial-grade fireworks. They ignited fires, hurled Molotov cocktails, destroyed barricades, smashed windows, and attacked individuals. An ordinary student protest had become an unmanageable riot, which continued into the city of Berkeley, overwhelming campus police and forcing cancellation of the event.[1] President Donald Trump then tweeted that Berkeley had infringed free speech and might lose federal funds.[2]

The transformation of heated controversies into violent events continued in March 2017, when a person was shot after Yiannopoulos spoke at the University of Washington, even though the campus spent almost $100,000 on extra security.[3] That same month, Professor Allison Stanger of Middlebury College was seriously injured when protestors, angry that Charles Murray had been invited to speak, attacked her and Murray while they were trying to leave the campus.[4] Sixty-seven students were later disciplined, although none were suspended or expelled.[5]

Matters became even more disturbing and tragic in late August 2017, when white nationalist Richard Spencer was scheduled to speak at a "Unite the Right" rally in Charlottesville, Virginia. The night before the rally, several hundred torch-bearing white nationalists marched on the main quadrangle of the University of Virginia grounds, shouting "you will not replace us" and "Jew will not replace us." When counter-protestors engaged the group, marchers threw their torches toward students and a brawl ensued.[6] The next day the groups converged, with self-styled militia members dressed in full camouflage and outfitted with semiautomatic rifles and pistols. Many white nationalists carried large shields and long wooden clubs. They charged through a line of counter-protestors, swinging sticks, punching, and spraying chemicals.

Not long after police ordered the groups to disperse, a member of the white nationalist group drove a car into a crowd, killing a counter-protestor named Heather Heyer.[7]

Soon after that incident, Spencer was able to speak at the University of Florida, but only after the campus made extensive security efforts and the governor declared a state of emergency.[8] Spencer also spoke at Auburn and Michigan State after federal judges prevented each university from denying him access; at MSU, 100 officers in riot gear broke up fights and made arrests.[9] Spencer initially sued the Ohio State University when that campus refused him access, but dropped the lawsuit when the campus sought evidence exploring whether Spencer was coordinating with others who were planning violence at the event. The university claimed that at previous events, Spencer and other event organizers "only feigned cooperation with local officials on safety matters while drawing up secret military-style plans to disobey law enforcement or campus directives if their event was limited in ways they deemed unacceptable."[10]

In the summer of 2017, conservative student groups announced that they would stage a "Free Speech Week" at UC Berkeley, to include provocative speakers such as Ben Shapiro, Milo Yiannopoulos, Steve Bannon, and Ann Coulter. Shapiro came and gave an address in a large campus auditorium, and Yiannopoulos appeared on campus for fifteen minutes. The rest of free speech week was canceled at the last minute by the student organizers. Nonetheless, Berkeley spent over $3.9 million for security for the anticipated events.[11]

These, of course, are just a few of the countless examples of what has occurred since we wrote this book.

These events do not change our basic argument. While campuses have vitally important obligations to create safe, inclusive, and nondiscriminatory learning environments, they cannot do so by censoring or punishing the mere expression of ideas. The vast majority of campus controversies do not involve large-scale events that pose risks of violence but more ordinary efforts to silence speech that some find disagreeable or offensive. More common than the controversies surrounding visits by Yiannopoulos and Spencer have been the efforts to prevent University of Oregon President Michael Schill from delivering his state of the university report, to prevent an ACLU attorney from speaking about free speech at the College of William and Mary, or to disrupt a meeting of College Republicans at UC Santa Cruz.[12] The most recent studies demonstrate that students continue to wrestle with how best to value free speech and inclusivity, with more than half of students valuing diversity and inclusivity above free speech, more than half supporting bans on hate speech, and almost a third supporting restrictions on offensive speech.[13] Our point in writing the book was to make the case for why the expression of opinion should not be censored or punished, especially on college campuses.

Still, this argument is now taking place in a context where some discourse has become much uglier and more hateful, and where violence is a legitimate concern. Campus-based controversies are being weaponized by outsiders who are more interested in creating dramatic confrontations than in anything resembling a dialogue.[14] Campuses are also facing unprecedented questions about whether there are limits to their obligations to spend money to provide security for such events.[15]

If we had imagined that campuses might find themselves regularly spending hundreds of thousands or even millions of dollars to protect controversial speakers, we would have addressed that question more fully. But our basic principles would not have changed. If the protection of speech imposes costs on public entities—for example, for accommodating tens of thousands of protestors for an anti-fascist and pro-diversity rally in Boston a week after the tragic Charlottesville demonstration—then those costs must be borne and cannot be imposed on the demonstrators as a condition of the exercise of their rights.[16] It is a violation of free speech norms to charge some groups more for the right to speak than others, merely because some views are more controversial and invite more counter-demonstrations—although it raises no concerns for campuses to charge organizers of large events the ordinary additional costs of hosting such an event (e.g., hiring additional parking attendants) compared to hosting smaller events.[17] It is unlikely that any entity will be forced to choose between its fundamental financial solvency and its free speech obligations, but until such a dramatic case arises, campuses should take inspiration from UC Berkeley's extraordinary efforts in 2017 and do all they can to ensure that free expression is not censored or disrupted by protestors.

Then again, as we argue in the book, campuses have the legal and ethical duty to protect the safety of students, staff, and faculty. Campuses must accommodate the battle of ideas but not actual battles. That certain ideas are considered inherently hateful or threatening cannot be the basis for censoring or punishing their mere expression. But we should not confuse the requirement to protect the expression of all ideas with the need to stand helpless when mobs gather to initiate or provoke violence. People do not enter campuses in large groups equipped with bats, helmets, shields, masks, pepper spray, and body armor to listen to a lecture. There is no constitutional right to bring guns or other weapons to a rally. There is no right to conspire with others to organize violent confrontations.

All of these observations are consistent with our position in this book. While the dramatic events of 2017 and early 2018 demonstrate that speech can have very serious consequences, they do not undermine basic arguments, forged over centuries, for the protection of free expression.

In Chapter 5 we offer our thoughts about what campuses can and cannot do with regard to speech. We use the occasion of this new Preface to offer campus leaders a checklist that will help them determine if they are prepared to address issues that are sure to arise at their colleges and universities.

AN "ARE YOU PREPARED?" CHECKLIST FOR CAMPUS LEADERS

You are prepared to address inevitable controversies about free speech and inclusivity if you:

1. Articulate and disseminate a clear statement of the fundamental importance of protecting free expression and create opportunities for members of the campus community to learn more about free speech.
2. Clarify in advance that the institution will support the presence on campus of individuals who hold dissenting or controversial views.

3. Develop rules for approving events that are clear and easy to find, and will be applied equally regardless of the viewpoint of a speaker or sponsoring group.

4. Ensure the safety of all, including the protection of the speaker's rights.

5. Publicize clear rules that prohibit disrupting the speech of others during authorized campus events, and provide for disciplinary measures when appropriate.

6. Take all steps necessary, short of prohibiting the expression of ideas, to create and maintain inclusive and nondiscriminatory learning environments for all students.

The reasoning underlying these recommendations is to be found in the following pages.

NOTES

1. Madison Park and Kyung Lah, *Berkeley Protests of Yiannapoulos Caused $100,000 in Damage*, CNN.COM (Feb. 2, 2017), https://www.cnn.com/2017/02/01/us/milo-yiannopoulos-berkeley/index.html.

2. Susan Svrluga and Brian Murphy, *Trump Lashes Back at Berkeley after Violent Protests Block Speech by Breitbart Writer Milo Yiannopoulos*, WASH. POST (Feb. 2, 2017), https://www.washingtonpost.com/news/grade-point/wp/2017/02/01/berkeley-cancels-speech-by-breitbart-writer-milo-amid-intense-protests/?utm_term=.04e50e71f00b.

3. Daniel Gilbert, *Milo Yiannopoulos at UW: A Speech, a Shooting and $75,000 in Police Overtime*, SEATTLE TIMES (March 26, 2017), https://www.seattletimes.com/seattle-news/crime/milo-yiannopoulos-at-uw-a-speech-a-shooting-and-75000-in-police-overtime/.

4. Allison Stanger, *Understanding the Angry Mob at Middlebury That Gave Me a Concussion*, N.Y. TIMES (March 13, 2017), https://www

.nytimes.com/2017/03/13/opinion/understanding-the-angry-mob-that-gave-me-a-concussion.html.

5. Stephanie Saul, *Dozens of Middlebury Students Are Disciplined for Charles Murray Protest*, N.Y. TIMES (May 24, 2017), https://www.nytimes.com/2017/05/24/us/middlebury-college-charles-murray-bell-curve.html.

6. Hawes Spencer and Sheryl Gay Stolberg, *White Nationalist March on University of Virginia*, N.Y. TIMES (Aug. 11, 2017), https://www.nytimes.com/2017/08/11/us/white-nationalists-rally-charlottesville-virginia.html.

7. Joe Heim, *Recounting a Day of Rage, Hate, Violence and Death*, WASH. POST (Aug. 14, 2017), https://www.washingtonpost.com/graphics/2017/local/charlottesville-timeline/?utm_term=.829170c4c067.

8. Matt Pearce and Les Neuhaus, *White Nationalist Richard Spencer to Noisy Florida Protestors: You Didn't Shut Me Down*, L.A. TIMES (Oct. 19, 2017), http://www.latimes.com/nation/la-na-florida-spencer-speech-20171019-story.html.

9. David Jesse and RJ Wolcott, *Fistfights, Arrests at Michigan State University before Richard Spencer Takes Stage*, DETROIT FREE PRESS (March 5, 2017), https://www.freep.com/story/news/local/michigan/2018/03/05/richard-spencer-michigan-state-university/395079002/, and Travis M. Andrews, *Federal Judge Stops Auburn from Canceling White Nationalist Richard Spencer Speech*, WASH. POST (April 19, 2017), https://www.washingtonpost.com/news/morning-mix/wp/2017/04/19/federal-judge-stops-auburn-from-canceling-white-nationalists-speech-violence-erupts/?utm_term=.e05e6dc2ecob.

10. *Richard Spencer to Drop Ohio State Lawsuit*, CINCINNATI.COM (March 6, 2018), https://www.cincinnati.com/story/news/2018/03/06/richard-spencer-drop-ohio-state-lawsuit/401291002/, and Lori Falce, *Ohio State Responds to Spencer Suit, Cites Safety as Reason for Denial*, CENTRE TIMES DAILY (Jan. 7, 2017), https://www.cincinnati.com/story/news/2018/03/06/richard-spencer-drop-ohio-state-lawsuit/401291002/.

11. Frances Dinkelspiel, *UC Berkeley Spent Close to $4m on Security in Just One Month in 2017*, BERKELEYSIDE (Feb. 6, 2018), http://www.berkeleyside.com/2018/02/06/uc-berkeley-spent-close-4m-security-just-one-month-2017.

12. Michael H. Schill, *The Misguided Student Crusade Against "Fascism,"* N.Y. TIMES (Oct. 23, 2017), https://www.nytimes.com/2017/10/23/opinion/fascism-protest-university-oregon.html, Jeremy Bauer-Wolf, *Free Speech Advocate Silenced,* INSIDE HIGHER ED (Oct. 6, 2017), https://www.insidehighered.com/news/2017/10/06/william-mary-students-who-shut-down-aclu-event-broke-conduct-code, and Jessica A. York, *UC Santa Cruz Protest at Republican Student Meeting Leads to Arrests,* SANTA CRUZ SENTINEL (Oct. 20, 2017), http://www.santacruzsentinel.com/article/NE/20171020/NEWS/171029947.

13. Niraj Chokshi, *What College Students Really Think About Free Speech,* N.Y. TIMES (March 12, 2018), https://www.nytimes.com/2018/03/12/us/college-students-free-speech.html, and Knight Foundation, FREE EXPRESSION ON CAMPUS: WHAT COLLEGE STUDENTS THINK ABOUT FIRST AMENDMENT ISSUES (March 11, 2018), https://www.knightfoundation.org/reports/free-expression-on-campus-what-college-students-think-about-first-amendment-issues.

14. Jennifer Delton, *When "Free Speech" Becomes a Political Weapon,* WASH. POST (Aug. 22, 2017), https://www.washingtonpost.com/news/made-by-history/wp/2017/08/22/when-free-speech-becomes-a-political-weapon/?utm_term=.abc664fa00ea, and Kalina Newman, *Why Hate Groups Target Campuses—And What to Do When They Show Up,* USA TODAY COLLEGE (Aug. 15, 2017), http://college.usatoday.com/2017/08/15/why-hate-groups-target-campuses-—-and-what-to-do-when-they-show-up/.

15. Caroline Simon, *Free Speech Isn't Free: It's Costing College Campuses Millions,* FORBES (Nov. 20, 2017), https://www.forbes.com/sites/carolinesimon/2017/11/20/free-speech-isnt-free-its-costing-college-campuses-millions/#1d6c96611ee7.

16. Kurtis Lee and Vera Haller, *"Thank God Nobody Got Hurt": Boston Protesters Gather Peacefully a Week after Charlottesville Violence,* L.A. TIMES (Aug. 19, 2017), http://www.latimes.com/nation/la-na-boston-march-20170819-story.html.

17. *Forsythe County, Georgia v. The Nationalist Movement,* 505 U.S. 123 (1992).

Preface

Controversies over freedom of speech on college campuses have existed as long as there have been college campuses. But the specific issues vary with each generation. In recent years the tension has been between the desire to protect the learning experience of all students and the desire to safeguard freedom of expression.

Students are rightly demanding, and colleges and universities are striving to provide, greater diversity and an environment conducive to learning for all students. Often, though, these efforts have led to calls by students and faculty members to restrict, punish, or disrupt speech that is seen as creating a hostile learning environment, especially for those who have traditionally suffered discrimination. Some of this anger has been focused on speech that almost anyone would consider offensive and hateful. But there have also been calls to suppress speech that is merely politically controversial or contrarian. There are demands that campuses deal with "microaggressions" and require faculty to provide "trigger warnings" before covering material that some students might find upsetting. Students have demanded—and received—formal investigations of possible violations of federal law after faculty members published scholarly articles in journals. The issues concerning speech on campus are complicated by the unprecedented ability for any person to quickly reach a large audience via social media.

As teachers and university administrators, we have a personal stake in the recent debate concerning freedom of speech on campuses. We fear that discussions over this issue, like so much else in society, are polarizing into two camps. One derides all efforts to protect students from the effects of offensive or disrespectful speech as "coddling" and "political correctness." The other side believes that free speech rights are secondary to the need to protect the learning experience of students, especially minority students.

We wrote this book because we believe that both sides are right—and wrong. They are right in that both equality of educational opportunity and freedom of speech are essential for colleges and universities. But they are wrong in thinking that one of these objectives can be pursued to the exclusion of the other. Colleges and universities must create inclusive learning environments for all students *and* protect freedom of speech. To achieve both of these goals, campuses may do many things, but they must not treat the expression of ideas as a threat to the learning environment. Freedom of expression and academic freedom are at the very core of the mission of colleges and universities, and limiting the expression of ideas would undermine the very learning environment that is central to higher education.

This book is our effort to describe, as specifically as possible, what campuses can and can't do, and should and shouldn't do, to achieve both of these goals. We recognize, of course, that the First Amendment applies only to public colleges and universities. But academic freedom—above all, the ability to express all ideas and viewpoints, no matter how offensive—is necessary at all colleges and universities. Freedom of expression therefore should be the same at all institutions of higher education. Throughout this book, we rely on First Amendment law in describing what public universities can and can't do. But we draw no distinction between public and private schools when arguing for what they *should* and *shouldn't* do.

Our focus is solely on colleges and universities. We realize that similar issues arise in high schools, junior high schools, and even elementary schools. But the Supreme Court has given these schools' administrators much more latitude to regulate student speech, and the norms of academic freedom are different, and more central, in higher education.

The issue of free speech on college campuses is as old as universities and as current as the daily news. We have written this book because we believe that colleges must promote inclusive learning environments in a way that also preserves and respects the unfettered expression of ideas on campus. This requires a renewed appreciation of the importance of both values, an explanation of why we should not allow one value to override the other, and a clear path forward for how to advance and defend each of these fundamental features of higher education.

CHAPTER ONE

The New Censorship

WHERE should we draw the line between protecting free speech on college campuses and protecting an inclusive learning environment? Hardly a week goes by without new tensions around this question.[1] Just in the year 2015, for instance, the following events occurred.

- In February, George "Trey" Barnett, a student at the University of Tulsa, was suspended because of statements his husband made on Facebook. Barnett's husband posted criticisms of other students and University of Tulsa staff members who were involved in a theater production with Barnett. After professor Susan Barrett filed a harassment complaint against Barnett because of the postings, administrators suspended him from his courses and campus activities and barred him from publicizing his situation. Barnett's husband signed a sworn affidavit that he, not Barnett, was solely responsible for the posts. Barnett was suspended two months before his scheduled graduation, kept from returning to campus for a year, and barred from seeking a degree in his major, musical theater.[2]

- Also in February, Northwestern professor Laura Kipnis wrote an article for the *Chronicle of Higher Education* titled "Sexual Paranoia Strikes Academe," in which she criticized what she called the "layers of prohibition and sexual terror" that have inspired campus rules prohibiting romantic relationships between professors and students. Kipnis wrote: "It's the fiction of the all-powerful professor embedded in the new campus codes that appalls me. . . . If this is feminism, it's feminism hijacked by melodrama. The melodramatic imagination's obsession with helpless victims and powerful predators is what's shaping the conversation of the moment, to the detriment of those whose interests are supposedly being protected, namely students. The result? Students' sense of vulnerability is skyrocketing."[3] She added that students "so committed to their own vulnerability, conditioned to imagine they have no agency, and protected from unequal power arrangements in romantic life" will struggle to deal with the problems and conflicts of the real world.[4]

Two women graduate students filed a complaint against Kipnis, stating that her article had created a hostile learning environment in violation of Title IX, which prohibits educational institutions receiving federal funds from discriminating based on sex. Kipnis was subjected to an investigation lasting several months but ultimately was not disciplined.[5]

- In March, members of the Sigma Alpha Epsilon fraternity at the University of Oklahoma were on a bus, dressed in formal wear, going to a fraternity event. Two students led the others in a racist chant:

  There will never be a nigger at SAE
  There will never be a nigger at SAE
  You can hang him from a tree
  But he'll never sign with me
  There never will be a nigger at SAE

  President David Boren expelled the two students who led the chant and suspended the fraternity from the campus.[6]

- In April, administrators at Youngstown State University ordered the removal of all posters promoting a "straight pride" week. These posters had been placed on university bulletin boards where all students are allowed to post whatever they please. Jack Fahey, the vice president for student affairs, wrote a memo: "As most of you know, an inappropriate flyer announcing 'Straight Pride Week' was posted throughout the campus yesterday. Student leaders were told to help by taking them down where they saw them."[7]

- In July, Texas Christian University upheld the suspension of student Harry Vincent for postings on his Facebook page and on Twitter that expressed conservative views on such topics as the threat of terrorism and the spread of the Islamic State. Some months earlier, a person who self-identified as "Kelsey," who lived in Maryland and was not a TCU student, went on social media and urged people to complain to TCU about Vincent's posts, some of which Kelsey felt were racist. Complaints were filed against Vincent with the university.[8]

In April, Vincent received a letter from TCU's associate dean of campus life, Glory Z. Robinson, charging him with violating provisions of the Student Conduct Code that prohibited "Infliction of Bodily or Emotional Harm" and "Disorderly Conduct."[9] Vincent was found to have violated the provisions and was given a "Suspension in Abeyance" and placed on "Disciplinary Probation" until his graduation from TCU. Under the terms of his suspension, he could be on campus only to attend his classes and could not reside on campus, participate in any co-curricular activities, or use any nonacademic facilities on campus. He was required to complete a course entitled "Issues in Diversity" and to do sixty hours of community service. He appealed this judgment, and in July, a campus appeals panel ruled against him and upheld the punishments. Student Conduct and Grievance Committee chair Lynn K. Flahive wrote in a letter to Vincent, "The choices you made caused harm to other individuals. These types of comments are not acceptable at TCU."[10]

- In October, UCLA suspended its chapters of the fraternity Sigma Phi Epsilon and the sorority Alpha Phi after they co-hosted a "Kanye Western"-themed party, with costumes imitating Kanye West and his wife, Kim Kardashian.[11] The student newspaper, the *Daily Bruin*, had urged these actions against the fraternity and sorority: "By hosting a 'Kanye Western'-themed raid, Sigma Phi Epsilon and Alpha Phi have brought UCLA Greek Life to national attention for the worst reason. The office of UCLA Fraternity and Sorority Relations must take action to ensure such an event doesn't occur again on our campus, and the university must recognize the need to prevent racist incidents that don't necessarily target, but nonetheless demeans UCLA's black community."[12]

- Shortly before Halloween, the Intercultural Affairs Committee at Yale University sent an email to students cautioning them against wearing costumes that could be perceived as "culturally unaware or insensitive."[13] Professor Nicholas Christakis and his wife, Erika, a lecturer in early childhood education, were co-masters (a term that has since been discarded) of one of Yale's residential colleges. In response to complaints by students about the university's trying to regulate their costumes, Erika sent an email to students saying students should enjoy the holiday and no person could set strict definitions around what is offensive or culturally "appropriative." She asked whether blond toddlers should be barred from being dressed as African American or Asian characters from Disney films. "Is there no room anymore," she wrote, "for a child or young person to be a little bit obnoxious . . . a little bit inappropriate or provocative or, yes, offensive? American universities were once a safe space not only for maturation but also for a certain regressive, or even transgressive, experience; increasingly, it seems, they have become places of censure and prohibition."[14]

In an incident that was videotaped and widely viewed, angry students confronted Nicholas Christakis and demanded that he and his wife resign.[15] Hundreds of Yale students signed a letter disagreeing with Erika Christakis's argument that "free speech and the ability to tolerate offence" should take precedence over other considerations. "To ask marginalized students to throw away their enjoyment of a holiday, in order to expend emotional, mental, and physical energy to explain why something is offensive, is—offensive," the letter said. "To be a student of color on Yale's campus is to exist in a space that was not created for you."[16]

In December, Erika Christakis announced that she would no longer teach at the university.[17]

- In November, Thaddeus Pryor was suspended by Colorado College for a comment he posted on the anonymous social media application Yik Yak. In a reply to the comment "#blackwomenmatter" on Yik Yak, Pryor wrote, "They matter, they're just not hot."[18]

    Colorado College found that Pryor's post violated its "Abusive Behavior" and "Disruption of College Activities" policies and suspended him from the college until August 28, 2017. He was barred from setting foot on campus and forbidden from taking classes at other institutions for academic credit.[19]

In 2016, we saw more of the same. Every month, if not every week, has brought additional instances of campuses being urged to punish students for their speech. In March and April, for example, some Donald Trump supporters accepted an invitation to participate in "The Chalkening," a plan to aggravate Trump opponents on college campuses by posting pro-Trump messages in chalk.[20] At several campuses—including Tulane and the University of California, San Diego—anti-Trump advocates demanded that the administration punish those responsible not just for slurs like "fuck Mexicans" (which deserve condemnation) but for expressing political views such as "Build That Wall."[21]

In August, University of Chicago dean of students John Ellison sent a letter to incoming freshmen stating, "Our commitment to academic freedom means that we do not support so-called trigger warnings, we do not cancel invited speakers because their topics might prove controversial, and we do not condone the creation of intellectual 'safe spaces' where individuals can retreat from ideas and perspectives at odds with their own."[22] The letter attracted widespread media coverage and both praise and sharp criticism.[23] Most notably, 152 staff members at the University of Chicago signed a letter criticizing Ellison. The staff members said that they "believe trigger warnings and safe spaces allow heated, intellectual discussions to take place, but in an atmosphere that guarantees that everyone, especially the usually marginalized people, are comfortable."[24]

In October 2016, a University of Oregon law professor was suspended for wearing blackface at a Halloween party held at her house.[25] She said that she was doing so to promote a conversation about race. Twenty-three law school faculty members wrote a letter urging the professor to resign. It concluded: "If you care about our students, you will resign. If you care about our ability to educate future lawyers, you will resign. If you care about our alumni, you will resign." The University of Oregon commissioned an investigation which concluded: "We find that Nancy Shurtz's costume, including what constitutes 'blackface' through use of black makeup, constitutes a violation of the University's policies against discrimination. We further find that the actions constitute Discriminatory Harassment."[26]

These and countless other examples show the pervasiveness of issues concerning freedom of speech on college campuses.[27] They are arising at public universities, where the First Amendment applies, and at private universities, where campus rules generally protect speech even though the First Amendment does not apply. Large schools and small schools, prestigious and less prestigious, urban and rural, all are experiencing this. Sometimes speech that physically occurs on campus is being punished, sometimes the expression is on social media. While student speech has attracted the most attention, expression by faculty members and even staff is hardly immune from calls for regulation and punishment.

OUR EXPERIENCE

A 2015 survey by Yale University's William F. Buckley Program showed that 72 percent of students support disciplinary action against "any student or faculty member on campus who uses language that is considered racist, sexist, homophobic or otherwise offensive."[28] We found this sentiment among our own students.

In the Winter 2016 quarter, we co-taught a seminar on freedom of speech on college campuses at the University of California, Irvine. We had fifteen undergraduate students, all freshmen. They were impressive, serious learners. We began each class by posing a real-world problem and polling their views, starting with the incident of the racist chant on the fraternity members' bus at the University of Oklahoma. We asked our class, "if the expelled students sued and claimed that their free speech rights were violated, who should prevail, the students or the university?" The students voted 15–0 in favor of the university; not one member of the class felt that the expelled fraternity members were engaged in speech protected by the First Amendment. All believed such racist speech is harmful and should be punished by campus officials.[29]

This experience was repeated throughout the quarter. On every problem, we found that the students, usually overwhelmingly, favored stopping and punishing offensive speech by faculty and students. They often spoke of the need to stop "microaggressions" and of the importance of creating "safe spaces" for students. Of course, we do not want to generalize from one class and one group of students. But their views are consistent with the William F. Buckley Program's national study and with the instances described above. We learned many things from teaching this class.

This generation has a strong and persistent urge to protect others against hateful, discriminatory, or intolerant speech, especially in educational settings.

This is the first generation of students educated, from a young age, not to bully. For as long as they can remember, their schools have organized "tolerance weeks." Our students often told stories of how bullying at school and on social media had affected people they cared about. They are deeply sensitized to the psychological harm associated with hateful or intolerant speech. Descriptions of this generation of students too often omit this sense of compassion and their admirable desire to protect their fellow students.

Arguments about the social value of freedom of speech are very abstract to them, because they did not grow up at a time when the act of punishing speech was associated with undermining other worthwhile values.

Our students knew little about the history of free speech in United States and had no awareness of how important free speech had been to vulnerable political minorities. The two of us grew up in the time of the civil rights movement and anti–

Vietnam War protests. We saw first hand how officials attempted to stifle or punish protestors in the name of defending community values or protecting the public peace. We also saw how free speech assisted the drive for desegregation, the push to end the war, and the efforts of historically marginalized people to challenge convention and express their identities in new ways. In our experience, speech that was sometimes considered offensive, or that made people uncomfortable, was a good and necessary thing. We have an instinctive distrust of efforts by authorities to suppress speech.

This historic link between free speech and the protection of dissenters and vulnerable groups is outside the direct experience of today's students, and it was too distant to affect their feelings about freedom of speech. They were not aware of how the power to punish speech has been used primarily against social outcasts, vulnerable minorities, and those protesting for positive change—the very people toward whom our students are most sympathetic. Their perception of speech is shaped more by internet vitriol than by the oppression of Eugene Debs, Anita Whitney, John Thomas Scopes, Jehovah's Witnesses who refused to say the Pledge of Allegiance, leftists during the McCarthy era, civil rights activists who were beaten and even killed, Lenny Bruce, draft card burners, or George Carlin. Their instinct is to trust the government, including the public university, to regulate speech to protect students and prevent disruptions of the educational environment.

The students agreed that campuses should not be cleansed of all controversial opinions or all expressions that some might consider offensive. Still, they remained unconvinced of the value of defending hateful or discriminatory speech. They acknowledged that one could adopt a "more speech" solution rather than an "enforced silence" or punishment solution, but they doubted that this would protect their peers from psychological distress.

Current debates about the appropriate boundaries of campus free speech are not a mere replay of 1990s debates over campus "hate speech" codes.

Obviously some of the incidents we have described involve hate speech, but many involve punishing speech because of the ideas expressed. We can confirm what the Pew Research Center reported in November 2015: this generation of college students is much more supportive of censoring offensive statements about minorities and much less supportive of protecting speech that makes some students uncomfortable.[30] Students are also much less open to countervailing arguments about the need to protect hateful or controversial speech.

As debates continue about the appropriate boundaries of free speech on campus, strong free speech advocates—and we place ourselves in this category—cannot assume that the social benefits of broad free speech protections will be automatically appreciated by a generation that has not itself struggled against censorship and punishment of protestors, dissenters, and iconoclasts. American history amply demonstrates that there is no natural or inevitable intuition to support disruptive, offensive, or even countercultural speech. The country has a much longer history of suppressing unpopular speakers than of protecting them. The pro–free speech case needs to be made anew, even as campuses redouble their efforts to ensure that all students, and especially those who have been traditionally underrepresented, feel protected and included.

The issue of free speech on campus, and when students and faculty can be punished for their expression, is obviously not new. But there are important ways in which it has changed. Very often in the past, especially in the 1960s and 1970s, campus free speech issues arose when administrators sought to restrict student protests. We think of the Berkeley Free Speech Movement, which occurred in the 1964–65 academic year, where a group of students led a protest against the ban of political activities on campus, against the requirement for loyalty oaths, and for the students' free speech rights.[31] We think of the anti–Vietnam War demonstrations, fueled by men who faced the draft, and administrators' efforts to stop the protests. We remember the protests that closed college campuses in the spring of 1970 and the tragic killing of four students by the National Guard at Kent State University on May 4, 1970.

Today, however, it is students who demand that the campus take action against speech they find offensive. This reflects not only the distinctive experiences and concerns of this generation of students, but also the changing demographics of American higher education. Campuses today are much more diverse than was the case when we were students. This means there are more people on campus who can testify to the very real harms associated with hateful or intolerant speech, or the day-to-day indignities of microaggressions. Those who experience or witness these harms often direct their anger at university officials for not taking sufficient action to protect people from speech that they see as creating a hostile learning environment.

The internet also has dramatically changed the nature of freedom of speech, and thus perceptions about it on college campuses. Any person with access to a computer or a smartphone can quickly reach a large audience, and any other person with similar access can get the information. The difficulty of suppressing speech transcends state and national boundaries. But by the same token, the internet and social media can be used to say offensive things to a large audience, to reveal private information, and to bully and harass.[32] In the era of the internet and social media, today's students cannot imagine that free expression could be lost, but they also realize that the omnipresence of these media in their lives makes it impossible to shut oneself off from hateful or offensive speech.

Many students associate free speech with bullying and shaming. Their sense of speech is not sit-ins at segregated lunch counters to bring about positive change. It is Yik Yak, which began as a smartphone application that allows people to anonymously create and view discussion threads within a five-mile radius. Because it has been used for bullying and harassment, a number of high schools have banned Yik Yak, and schools such as Emory University and Wesleyan University have tried to prohibit it.[33] Social media make students think immediately of the harms, not the benefits, of speech.

Another difference is that some students extend the language of "harm" and "threat" to apply not only to traditional examples of so-called hate speech, but also to the expression of any idea they see as contrary to their strongly held views of social justice. More than in the 1990s, some students expect that a supportive campus environment is one in which their views are not challenged. We have heard of many instances of students walking out of class when other students say things they disagree with, and then demanding protection from the threat of having to listen to such views. The students at Northwestern complained about Laura Kipnis not because she used an ugly epithet, but because she criticized a campus policy that prohibited sexual relationships between faculty and students. The demand to punish those who wrote in chalk "Trump Build that Wall" came because it was a controversial policy idea that was seen as disrespectful of immigrant students.

The U.S. Department of Education's Office of Civil Rights (OCR), and how it interprets campuses' obligations under Title VI and Title IX to ensure a nondiscriminatory learning environment, also contributes to the difference.[34] At times, the OCR seems to foster a sense that the expression of offensive ideas is a form of harassment. At the very least, it has provided students with a rights-based vocabulary for demanding formal investigations of speakers on the grounds that their politically controversial speech creates a "discriminatory learning environment." The complaint against Laura Kipnis is one example. Another occurred on our campus.

Each spring at the University of California, Irvine, campus groups such as Students for Justice in Palestine and the Muslim Student Union bring in speakers who are very critical of Israel. At times unquestionably anti-Semitic things have been said. The Zionist Organization of America filed a complaint with the Office of Civil Rights alleging that by allowing such speech to take place, the university was creating a hostile learning environment for Jewish students. The investigation took months and ultimately concluded that there was no basis for finding that there was a hostile or intimidating environment for Jewish students on campus. "There is insufficient evidence," the investigators wrote, "to support the complainant's allegation that the University failed to respond promptly and effectively to complaints by Jewish students that they were harassed and subjected to a hostile environment."[35] They added, "In the university environment, exposure to such robust and discordant expressions, even when personally offensive and hurtful, is a circumstance that a reasonable student in higher education may experience."[36] Although the campus was exonerated, it is still remarkable that the expression of ideas was by itself a sufficient basis for a complaint and a long investigation.

The OCR's decision to open an investigation of the University of Mary Washington in late 2015, on the ground that the university failed to monitor the anonymous social media platform Yik Yak, also has First Amendment implications. To compound matters, when the university's president, Richard Hurley, refuted the accusations against the university citing (among other considerations) free speech concerns, the students amended their complaint to the OCR accusing the president of violating Title IX by retaliating against them with a "disparaging letter." This echoes what happened in the Kipnis investigation, when a Title IX retaliation complaint was filed against the faculty member who accompanied Kipnis to her investigation because he told the faculty senate of his concerns about the process.[37]

We have been here before. In 2003, campus officials raised concerns that OCR was encouraging or requiring campuses to adopt speech codes that had previously been deemed unconstitutional. OCR issued a letter clarifying that it has no power to force universities to police speech that is protected by the First Amendment and that public universities could not ban merely offensive speech. Assistant Secretary of Education Gerald A. Reynolds acknowledged that "Some colleges and universities have interpreted OCR's prohibition of 'harassment' as encompassing all offensive speech regarding sex, disability, race, and other classifications."[38] But the First Amendment, he continued, prohibits the government from defining harassment as equivalent to "the mere expression of views, words, symbols or thoughts that some person finds offensive. Under OCR's standard, the conduct must also be considered sufficiently serious to deny or limit a student's ability to participate in or benefit from the educational program." Conduct would be evaluated using the standard of a "reasonable person" of the alleged victim's age and position, not simply the complainant's subjective view.[39]

Despite this clarification, OCR's recent decision to instruct the University of New Mexico to punish unwelcome "verbal conduct" of a sexual nature raises concerns that it is once again focusing on climate at the expense of the First Amendment.[40] It has been almost fifteen years since OCR reassured the community of its understanding of free speech protections,[41] and its recent actual and threatened investigations certainly add to the concern over free speech on college campuses.

HOW TO RESPOND?

We find much of what is said about free speech on college campuses unsatisfying. We are deeply troubled by the efforts to suppress and punish the expression of unpopular ideas. Those who call for punishment of speech that makes students feel uncomfortable fail to recognize the importance of speech and the danger in giving the government the power to regulate it.

But at the same time, much of the criticism of current students and their sensibilities fails to reflect the laudable compassion that motivates them. Greg Lukianoff and Jonathan Haidt, in a cover story published in the *Atlantic* titled "The Coddling of the American Mind," warn that accommodating students' concerns can even undermine their mental health.[42] "Vindictive protectiveness," they write, "prepares [students] poorly for professional life, which often demands intellectual engagement with people and ideas one might find uncongenial or wrong. The harm may be more immediate, too. A campus culture devoted to policing speech and punishing speakers is likely to engender patterns of thought that are surprisingly similar to those long identified by cognitive behavioral therapists as causes of depression and anxiety. The new protectiveness may be teaching students to think pathologically."[43]

But mocking these students or treating their concerns as pathological misses the mark. It is hardly a constructive approach to the tensions over offensive speech on college campuses. Nor is the response that students should "suck it up" and deal with it, which harkens back to a thankfully bygone age when racial and ethnic slurs were more common, disrespect of women was more acceptable, LGBT people were ridiculed and tormented, and teachers and coaches routinely used shaming to discourage poor performance.

Society is better now, and students are right to expect empathy for victims of hate and intolerance. Telling them to "toughen up" does not address their laudable desire to create a campus that is inclusive and conducive for learning by all students. Words can cause real harm and interfere with a person's education. Campuses have the duty to act—sometimes legally, always morally—to protect their students from injury. The challenge is to develop an approach to free speech on campus that both protects expression and respects the need to make sure that a campus is a conducive learning environment for all students.

OUR APPROACH

Our central thesis is that all ideas and views should be able to be expressed on college campuses, no matter how offensive or how uncomfortable they make people feel. But there are steps that campuses can and should take to create inclusive communities where all students feel protected. We will develop this thesis over the next five chapters.

Chapter 2 focuses on the importance of free speech. We were surprised by how little our students had thought about why freedom of expression is a fundamental right and why it must be protected. Any analysis of free speech on college campuses must begin with this.

Chapter 3 discusses the special role of free expression at colleges and universities. However important free speech principles are in society as a whole, they require even stronger protections in academic settings. Our position is absolute: campuses never can censor or punish the expression of ideas, however offensive, because otherwise they cannot perform their function of promoting inquiry, discovery, and the dissemination of new knowledge. Although the First Amendment applies only to public universities, *all* colleges and universities should commit themselves to these values.

In Chapter 4 we turn to the issue of hate speech on campus. We look at the real harms caused by hate speech on campus, review the First Amendment law in this area and the history of hate speech codes, and explain why we believe that although well intentioned, campus bans on hate speech are not desirable.

In Chapter 5 we focus on how to create inclusive learning environments without undermining freedom of speech. We have tried to describe as specifically as possible what campuses can and should do, and can't and shouldn't do, when it comes to regulating speech. They cannot and should not punish speech because it is offensive. But certain speech can be punished: true threats, harassment, destruction of property, and disruptions of classes and campus activities. Campuses can create time, place, and manner restrictions that protect the learning environment while also protecting free expression. Moreover—and this is too often forgotten—campus leaders can engage in more speech, proclaiming the type of community they seek and condemning speech that is inconsistent with it.

Finally, Chapter 6 looks to the future. The high-stakes debate over free speech on campuses, and the desire to protect students from offense, is not going away. Ultimately it is about whether campuses can be places that protect the learning experiences of all students as well as freedom of speech and academic freedom. Colleges and universities cannot succeed at their mission unless they find a way to do both. If campus leaders allow calls for "safe spaces" to suppress the expression of ideas, little will remain of free speech or academic inquiry. But if campus leaders do not find ways to create a conducive learning environment for everyone, they will discover that they have provided free speech to some but not to all.

CHAPTER TWO

Why Is Free Speech Important?

THE controversy over free speech on campuses can be understood only in the context of the history of free speech. In the United States, that context is inseparable from the First Amendment.

Freedom of expression—which includes verbal and nonverbal behaviors that express a person's opinion, point of view, or identity—is considered a fundamental right within our political system. The Supreme Court has called it "the matrix, the indispensable condition, of nearly every other form of freedom"[1] and has ruled that it occupies a "preferred place"[2] in our constitutional scheme.

Such phrases reflect the assumption within American constitutional law that speech claims should be treated as weightier than the reasons typically used to justify the suppression or punishment of speech. In other words, before the debate even starts, speech has an advantage, even against some very good reasons to limit it.

And there may be good reasons to limit speech. It has been used to mock and bully, and to question the dignity of entire groups of people in ways that put them at risk. It has been used to objectify women, sexualize children, and glorify violence. Speech can invade privacy or ruin a reputation. People have said or published things that threaten national security. Speech can fuel hatred among people, and—as we have seen all too often recently—it can incite people to commit horrific acts of violence against innocents.

There is constant tension between free speech and other values—national security, safety, public morality, privacy, reputation, dignity, equality. The current debate about free speech on college campuses is one example of a long-standing discussion of the best way to reconcile these competing considerations.

Yet despite the real and potential harms and risks, we believe that freedom of expression is an indispensable condition of all other freedoms and deserves a preferred place in our system.

Why believe this?

The history of freedom of speech in the United States provides a longer answer. But first we want to mention the three most common moral and practical reasons why expressive activity deserves broad protection: freedom of speech is essential to freedom of thought; it is essential to democratic self-government; and the alternative—government censorship and control of ideas—has always led to disaster.[3]

Freedom of Thought

First, freedom of speech is essential to freedom of thought because a person cannot develop an independent point of view about the world unless he or she is exposed to different ideas about what is important and what beliefs are most meaningful, and is permitted to converse with others about their experiences or beliefs. Just as totalitarian societies are premised on complete control over people's actions and beliefs, free societies are premised on freedom of thought and freedom of conscience—the right to have beliefs without risking punishment for "thoughtcrime" (the holding of unapproved beliefs and ideas).[4] This freedom can develop only in a society that protects a broad and diverse range of opinion.

This protection is necessary not for those whose beliefs and actions are consistent with dominant opinion (people seldom try to oppress what is accepted and popular), but for those who insist on asserting their individuality against dominant opinion. As Justice Oliver Wendell Holmes put it, "If there is any principle of the Constitution that more imperatively calls for attachment than any other it is the principle of free thought—not free thought for those who agree with us but freedom for the thought that we hate."[5] In this sense, free speech and freedom of thought are essential components of any truly diverse society. Without them, the pressure for conformity will overwhelm potential iconoclasts and outcasts, and there will be no true diversity of experiences, perspectives, or identities within the community.

Moreover, there is little value in allowing people to develop their own conscience, their own commitments, and their own identities if the society then criminalizes the ability to express them to others. To hide who you are and what you believe, for fear that the mere act of expressing yourself risks punishment, is an exceedingly cruel and oppressive circumstance. The rights of conscience and free expression are designed to prevent such a torment.

Free Speech and Democracy

Second, freedom of speech is essential to democratic self-government because democracy presupposes that the people may freely receive information and opinion on matters of public interest and the actions of government officials. The act of voting still occurs in many autocratic societies where speech is severely limited and government officials punish people who criticize the government. Many dictators brag about receiving over 90 percent of the vote, not realizing that such numbers cast doubt on their own validity. It is not the act of voting that creates a self-governing society but rather the people's ability to formulate and communicate their opinions about what decisions or policies will best advance the community's welfare. The right to be informed about matters of public interest is considered so fundamental to democracy that Benjamin Franklin called it the "principal pillar of a free government."[6] As Thomas Jefferson put it, "Were it left to me to decide whether we should have a government without newspapers, or newspapers without a government, I should not hesitate a moment to prefer the latter."[7]

Another way of saying this is that freedom of expression is the major bulwark against tyranny in any political system. All successful autocrats start by punishing dissenters, criminalizing speech that might threaten their power, and dominating those institutions that would otherwise be dedicated to incubating independent thought—including newspapers and (especially) universities. A citizenry that is not free to share its common experiences and hear dissenting views is hard-pressed to challenge those who oppress and immiserate them.

In free societies, meanwhile, rights of free expression allow a diverse political community to work through its different views without always succumbing to violence. Political systems are more stable when individuals feel as if they have had a fair chance to have their say, and even if they lose in the short run, will have more opportunities to convince their fellow citizens of the wisdom of their views.

Censorship and Society

Third, history shows that the alternative to freedom of speech—government censorship and control of ideas—is disastrous for a society. These methods have been used throughout history to prevent challenges to people in power, to secure the place of dominant social groups against people considered less worthy of respect, and to prevent the circulation of new ideas that are the essential engine of social progress. To make progress in our thinking about important matters, we need an extraordinary amount of tolerance for wrong hypotheses and strange-sounding ideas, because (as Steven Pinker observes), "everything we know about the world—the age of our civilization, species, planet, and universe; the stuff we're made of;

the laws that govern matter and energy; the workings of the body and brain—came as insults to the sacred dogma of the day."[8]

If one does not know the history of the struggle for free speech, one might think that restrictions on speech can be a force for protecting the vulnerable. But history tells us the exact opposite: censorship has always been on the side of authoritarianism, conformity, ignorance, and the status quo, and advocates for free speech have always been on the side of making societies more democratic, more diverse, more tolerant, more educated, and more open to progress.

This helps us understand why the protection of free speech has been so rare in human history, and is still rare today. Support for free speech is synonymous with a genuine commitment to democracy, diversity, and change. If you value social order and conformity more highly than you value liberty and democracy, then you will not support free speech no matter what else we say. Unfortunately, the prevailing stance of most political systems has been authoritarian, and the prevailing organization of most societies has favored rigid views about how people should behave. Free speech as an idea has developed—slowly, tenuously, over many centuries—only when there have been opportunities to break down more authoritarian and homogeneous structures of government and society. Free speech thrives when members of society agree that individuals should be free to make their own choices about what to believe and how to behave. It thrives when people agree that they should be able to challenge government leaders and advocate for social change. It is valued when people are open to new ideas about how the world works, how society should be organized, and what values are most important.

The history of free speech in America illustrates these points and provides an essential backdrop to today's debate over free speech on college campuses.

FREE SPEECH IN AMERICA BEFORE THE TWENTIETH CENTURY

There is some evidence that ideas of free speech existed during the short reign of Athenian democracy some 2,500 years ago, and among some leading orators of the troubled Roman Republic. But the first major free speech controversies in western history occurred in England, during the debates over the so-called Licensing Acts of 1643 and 1662, and these debates shaped the views of the generation that ratified the First Amendment to the United States Constitution.

Earlier, in the fifteenth century, European political and social elites had to come to grips with the creation of the printing press, which for the first time made it easy to circulate information and ideas without going through the existing hierarchy of the church and monarchy. The immediate response of the Roman Catholic Church was to impose severe restrictions on the use of the printing press. Pope Alexander VI, explaining in 1501 that the printing press could be "very harmful if it is permitted to widen the influence of pernicious works," determined that "full control over the printers" was necessary.[9] He required that a person obtain an official "license" from a proper authority in order to distribute materials printed on a printing press. If one wanted to print copies of the Bible, one would receive a license. If one was interested in printing works of dissent or criticism, the license would be denied.

In the spirit of the times, the English Licensing Acts of the 1600s required all persons to obtain official permission before publishing any material, and required the licenser to attest that the manuscript did not criticize Christianity or the government.[10]

The printing press forced political and social elites to make it clear that people could express themselves only if they did not challenge political and social elites. But it also led to the revolutionary idea that the publication of dissent and criticism should be tolerated rather than punished or censored.

The first great expression of this idea came from John Milton, the author of *Paradise Lost*, whose 1644 pamphlet *Areopagitica* is the seminal statement on free speech rights in Anglo-American history. Written just as the English Civil War was heating up, at a time when there were many challenges to existing political and religious authority, Milton (who sided with the Puritans against Charles I and the Church of England) emphasized the value of free speech for discovering truths. He used this argument to explain why it was not appropriate for the government to predetermine what ideas were and were not acceptable for free human beings to hear.[11]

Milton's most famous passage focused on how the licensing laws would have the effect of discouraging "all learning" and undermine the ability of people to understand truth:

> Though all the winds of doctrine were let loose to play upon the earth, so Truth be in the field, we do injuriously by licensing and prohibiting to misdoubt her strength. Let her and Falsehood grapple; who ever knew Truth put to

the worst in a free and open encounter? . . . [Since] the
knowledge and survey of vices is in this world so necessary
to the constituting of human virtue, and the scanning of
error to the confirmation of truth, how can we more safely,
and with less danger, scout into the regions of sin and fal-
sity than by reading all manner of tractates and hearing all
manner of reason?[12]

An important assumption underlying Milton's view is that individual persons should be respected enough to decide for
themselves whether a particular view was worthy of their support. Rather than have the government decide in advance
what was or was not truthful or worthy of attention, Milton,
like many English political and religious reformers of the
time, wanted that authority given to every person. In support
of this view he beseeched the "Lords and Commons of England" to treat their subjects not as "slow and dull, but of a
quick, ingenious and piercing spirit, acute to invent, subtle
and sinewy to discourse, not beneath the reach of any point
the highest that human capacity can soar to."[13]

Parliament refused to renew the Licensing Act when it
expired in 1694. By the middle of the eighteenth century,
both English and American authorities agreed that freedom
of the press meant that government could not pass what became known as "prior restraints." Moveover, increasing numbers of Enlightenment thinkers began to advocate for a world
that was more democratic, more tolerant of diverse views, and
more supportive of free inquiry. John Locke's "A Letter Concerning Toleration" (1689) made the case that the government should tolerate the proliferation of different religious
practices rather than force everyone to accept only the official

religion, and this helped set the stage for broader arguments about freedom of conscience.[14] In the early 1700s prominent English dissenters John Trenchard and Thomas Gordon, writing a series of "letters" under the pseudonym Cato, attacked what they considered to be the increasing corruption of British politics and made a special point in their essay "Of Freedom of Speech" to build on Milton's views:

> Without freedom of thought, there can be no such thing as wisdom; and no such thing as public liberty, without freedom of speech: Which is the right of every man, as far as by it he does not hurt and control the right of another. . . . That men ought to speak well of their governors, is true, while their governors deserve to be well spoken of; but to do public mischief, without hearing of it, is only the prerogative and felicity of tyranny: A free people will be showing that they are so, by their freedom of speech.[15]

While the founders of the American Republic agreed that licensing acts created too strong a choke hold on the expression of innovative or dissenting ideas, they also believed that society had a right to protect itself against dangerous speech. This had become the dominant opinion in English law at the time the U.S. Constitution was written. As the English legal commentator William Blackstone put it in his *Commentaries*, "Every freeman has an undoubted right to lay what sentiments he pleases before the public . . . but if he publishes what is improper, mischievous, or illegal, he must take the consequence of his own temerity."[16] In the language of constitutional law, prior restraints were prohibited but not "subsequent punishment" of bad speech.

What speech was "improper, mischievous, or illegal"? The main category of speech that could lead to punishment was "seditious libel," with "sedition" meaning an act designed to subvert lawful authority and "libel" defined as an expression that undermines reputation or brings someone or something into hatred or contempt.[17] Seditious libel was thus a statement or writing about the government or a government official—whether true or false—that would undermine authority and perhaps lead to a breach of the peace. While the American founders disagreed over whether truthful criticisms of the government deserved protection, most believed that "false, scandalous, and malicious" criticism should be punished.

This is one of the reasons why, despite the ratification of the First Amendment just a few years earlier, Congress could pass the Alien and Sedition Acts in 1798, making it harder for an immigrant to become a citizen, allowing the president to imprison or deport noncitizens who were deemed dangerous, and criminalizing false statements that were critical of the federal government.[18] Because the presidency and the Congress were at the time controlled by the Federalist Party, the prohibition against criticizing the government was most enforced against members of the opposition Democratic-Republican Party, led by Thomas Jefferson and James Madison. Using the law, the Adams administration shut down several prominent Jeffersonian newspapers, imprisoned Jeffersonian members of Congress, and even arrested Benjamin Franklin's grandson for libeling President Adams.

In the end, the partisan prosecutions generated enough outrage that the Federalists lost control of the federal government in 1800. After Jefferson became president, he allowed the Sedition Act to expire and pardoned those who had been convicted.

As a result of the controversy surrounding the Sedition Act, notions of free speech rights further developed to shield more people who criticized the government or government officials. But throughout the nineteenth century, United States law still allowed censorship or prosecution of people who engaged in "dangerous or offensive writings."

The most dramatic and important example of this censorship involved anti-slavery advocacy. When abolitionists in the 1830s began insisting on the emancipation of slaves, slaveholders decried their speech as dangerous because it might incite slave rebellions. Some efforts to silence anti-slavery advocacy took the form of mob justice, destroying abolitionist presses and murdering the editors of abolitionist journals. But the censors also used the power of law. While Northern states refused to formally punish abolitionist advocacy, Southern states made it a crime for anyone to express an anti-slavery position.[19] When the American Anti-Slavery Society mailed abolitionist pamphlets to prominent Southern citizens in 1835, Amos Kendell, the U.S. postmaster general, informed local postmasters that they had no obligation to deliver abolitionist literature, explaining that the federal government had a responsibility to protect "States from domestic violence."[20]

The other prominent nineteenth-century example of the suppression of speech was the passage of the Comstock Law in 1873. Pushed by groups such as the New York Society for the Suppression of Vice (led by Anthony Comstock), the law targeted the "Trade in and Circulation of, obscene literature and Articles for immoral use" and made it illegal to send any "obscene, lewd or lascivious" materials or any information or "any article or thing" related to contraception or abortion through the mail. The passage of the federal law encouraged many states to add laws of their own, and heavy-handed restrictions on contraceptive information and sexually oriented materials continued for many years.

Working as an unpaid special agent of the U.S. Post Office from 1874 until 1915, Comstock presided over the confiscation of some 130,000 pounds of obscene literature and 194,000 lewd pictures and photos. Among the works that would eventually fall under the Act's censorship net were Aristophanes' *Lysistrata*, Chaucer's *Canterbury Tales*, and books by Ernest Hemingway, Honoré de Balzac, Oscar Wilde, F. Scott Fitzgerald, Eugene O'Neill, and John Steinbeck. James Joyce's *Ulysses* was banned in the United States throughout the 1920s after the New York Society for the Suppression of Vice had the work declared obscene. Not until the 1930s, after the development of greater protections for speech and the press, did a court declare the book to be protected by the First Amendment.[21]

By the end of the nineteenth century it was acknowledged that people should have the freedom to criticize the government, government officials, and candidates for office, and to express a range of views on matters of public debate. Yet it was still commonplace to allow the censorship or punishment of speech that was considered "blasphemous," that harmed the reputation of a private individual, or (most expansively) that had a "tendency" to injure "public morals or safety." This last category in particular gave the government extraordinary opportunities to prosecute people for expressing unpopular or dissenting opinions, as became dramatically clear at the turn of the twentieth century.

HOLMES AND BRANDEIS IN DISSENT

In the years leading up to World War I,[22] many Americans feared that the new wave of immigrants from eastern and southern Europe would bring "anti-American" practices and ideas into the country, including socialism and anarchism. These fears were heightened when anarchists at the turn of the century assassinated several heads of state (including President William McKinley in 1901), the Socialist Party in the United States gained an increasing share of the vote in many urban communities, and militant labor leaders threatened mass strikes. Even before the United States entered the war, many Americans were calling for legislation to restrict "disloyal" utterances, usually associated with immigrants. In his State of the Union address in 1915, Woodrow Wilson warned that the increasing presence of American citizens who were "born under other flags" and "have poured the poison of disloyalty into the very arteries of our national life" was making it "necessary that we should promptly make use of the processes of law by which we may be purged of their corrupt distempers."[23]

Views such as these inspired the passage of the Espionage Act of 1917, the Sedition Act of 1918, and many similar state statutes. The Espionage Act made it a federal crime for a person to make a false report that attempted to cause insubordination, disloyalty, mutiny, or refusal of duty, including obstruction of the draft. The Sedition Act extended the range of offenses to cover speech that cast the government or the war effort in a negative light or interfered with the sale of government bonds. It forbade the use of "disloyal, profane, scurrilous, or abusive language" about the United States government, its flag, or its armed forces, or that caused others to view the American government or its institutions with contempt, and it allowed the postmaster general to refuse to deliver mail containing such language.[24]

Following passage of these laws, more than two thousand persons were arrested for violating federal restrictions on speech, and more than a thousand were convicted. They generally received sentences of five to twenty years' imprisonment.

In sustaining these convictions, the United States Supreme Court initially relied on traditional understandings of government power to regulate speech. *Schenck v. United States* (1919) turned on the question of whether Charles Schenck, the general secretary of the American Socialist Party, had a right to distribute pamphlets condemning the Wilson administration and arguing that the draft was unconstitutional.[25] Among other things, the pamphlet urged readers, "Do Not Submit to Intimidation" and "Assert Your Rights." Schenck was arrested, charged with violating the Espionage Act, and sentenced to ten years in prison. In upholding his conviction, Justice Oliver Wendell Holmes asserted:

> The most stringent protection of free speech would not protect a man in falsely shouting fire in a theatre and causing a panic. . . . The question in every case is whether the words are used in such circumstances and are of such a nature as to create a clear and present danger that they will bring about substantive evils that Congress has a right to prevent. . . . It seems to be admitted that if an actual obstruction of the recruiting service were proved, liability for words that produced that effect might be enforced.[26]

On this view, just as the government had the power to prosecute people for physically obstructing the draft, it also had the power to prosecute people for using words that had the same effect.

That decision was announced on March 3, 1919. A week later, the Court sustained the conviction of the prominent Socialist leader Eugene V. Debs—who had expressed admiration for three draft evaders and had told a crowd that "you need to know that you are for something better than slavery and cannon fodder"—also under the Espionage Act. Holmes again wrote the majority opinion; this time he asserted that persons could be constitutionally convicted when "the words used had as their natural tendency and reasonably probable effect to obstruct the recruiting services."[27]

The Red Scare that followed World War I inspired continued restrictions on political dissent, especially the advocacy of socialist or anarchist views. In April 1919, authorities discovered a plot for mailing thirty-six bombs to prominent political and business leaders, including J. P. Morgan, John D. Rockefeller, Justice Oliver Wendell Holmes, and Attorney General A. Mitchell Palmer. On June 2, 1919, eight bombs simultaneously exploded in eight different locations, including Palmer's house. Afterward, Palmer ordered what became known as the "Palmer Raids," a lawless dragnet designed to capture, arrest, and deport radical leftists from the United States. Over 10,000 persons were arrested; 556 were eventually deported.[28]

Many establishment figures felt that Palmer had gone too far. One result of their outrage was the founding of the American Civil Liberties Union, which published a *Report Upon the Illegal Practices of the United States Department of Justice.*[29]

Prominent legal scholars also began to write treatises advocating for a better approach to free speech protections.[30]

At this point, two Supreme Court justices began to articulate a different understanding of free speech rights. Through a series of dissenting opinions, Justice Oliver Wendell Holmes—who just months earlier had upheld the prosecution of dissenters—and Justice Louis Brandeis began a revolution in the thinking and practice of free speech rights in the United States.[31]

They started late in 1919, in a case where a majority of Supreme Court justices ruled that Jacob Abrams could be sentenced to ten years for urging American workers to protest American intervention against the Bolsheviks in the Russian Revolution.[32] The most famous passage of Holmes and Brandeis' dissent in *Abrams v. United States* asserted the following:

> Persecution for the expression of opinions seems to me perfectly logical. If you have no doubt of your premises or your power and want a certain result with all your heart you naturally express your wishes in law and sweep away all opposition. . . . But when men have realized that time has upset many fighting faiths, they may come to believe even more than they believe the very foundations of their own conduct that the ultimate good desired is better reached by a free trade of ideas—that the best test of truth is the power of the thought to get itself accepted in the competition of the market, and that truth is the only ground upon which their wishes safely can be carried out. That, at any rate, is the theory of our Constitution. . . . We should be eternally vigilant against attempts to check the expression of opinions that we loathe and believe to be fraught with death, unless they so imminently threaten immediate interference with the lawful and pressing purposes of the law that an immediate check is required to save the country.[33]

When it comes to restricting or punishing speech, in other words, it was not enough for the government to think that certain expressions have a "tendency" to cause bad outcomes. The traditional "bad tendency" basis for limiting speech meant, as a practical matter, that there could be no protection for controversial speech. Holmes and Brandeis argued that any concerns over the harmful effects of speech should be addressed by the "marketplace of ideas"—that is, by people exercising their speech rights to expose the harmful idea's dangers—rather than by government censorship or punishment. The major exception to this rule involved speech that created an "imminent threat" of lawlessness or real danger, such that there was no time for "more speech" to solve the problem (as with, for example, falsely shouting fire in a crowded theater in order to start a panic).

Brandeis reinforced this approach in his opinion in *Whitney v. California* (1927).[34] The case involved Charlotte Anita Whitney, an organizer with the California branch of the Communist Labor Party. She had advocated peaceful political change, but was convicted under the California Criminal Syndicalism Act of 1919 because of her association with the Communist Party. A majority of Supreme Court justices agreed that her actions presented a "danger to the public peace and the security of the State."[35] Brandeis disagreed. "Fear of serious injury," he wrote,

> cannot alone justify suppression of free speech and assembly. Men feared witches and burnt women. It is the function of speech to free men from the bondage of irrational fears. To justify suppression of speech there must be a reasonable ground to fear that serious evil will result if free speech is practiced. There must be reasonable ground to

believe that the danger apprehended is imminent. There must be reasonable ground to believe that the evil to be prevented is a serious one. . . . If there be time to expose through discussion the falsehood and fallacies, to avert the evil by the processes of education, the remedy to be applied is more speech, not enforced silence. Only an emergency can justify repression. Such must be the rule if authority is to be reconciled with freedom.[36]

This claim—that in almost every circumstance the best approach to combat the potential harm of speech "is more speech, not enforced silence"—has become the most common argument used by free speech advocates in response to those today who urge censorship and punishment of speech considered offensive or harmful.[37]

THE BENEFICIARIES OF
FREE SPEECH PROTECTION

Over the next half century, judges and civil libertarians worked to move American culture and practices toward the views expressed by Holmes and Brandeis in dissent. It was not a steady march of progress, and the full story is long and complicated. Today, judges and analysts still struggle and disagree over how to balance free speech against other important interests.

Yet between the 1930s and 1970s there was a revolution in thinking and practice about freedom of expression in the United States. Not surprisingly, the most important beneficiaries of this new conception of free speech were the most vulnerable members of society and those who most strongly advocated for social change, especially labor unions, religious minorities, political radicals, civil rights demonstrators, antiwar protestors, and nonconformists.

In 1937 the Supreme Court ruled that states could not prosecute people merely for belonging to the Communist Party or speaking at public meetings sponsored by the Communist Party.[38] That same year, Justice Benjamin Cardozo became the first justice to characterize freedom of speech as "the matrix, the indispensable condition, of nearly every other form of freedom."[39] During World War II this newly indispensable liberty was invoked to prevent states from punishing the children of Jehovah's Witnesses for refusing to pledge allegiance to the American flag. As Justice Robert Jackson explained in *West Virginia Board of Education v. Barnette* (1943), "If there is any fixed star in our constitutional constellation, it is that no official, high or petty, can prescribe what shall be orthodox in politics, nationalism, religion, or other matters of opinion or force citizens to confess by word or act their faith therein."[40] In *Keegan v. United States* (1945), the Court also ruled that persons could not be convicted of obstructing the draft merely for counseling others that the draft was unconstitutional—exactly the offense that sent Charles Schenck to jail in 1918.[41] By 1945, the justices were talking about "the preferred place given in our scheme to the great, indispensable democratic freedoms secured by the First Amendment."[42]

But there were dramatic setbacks in the protection of free speech. In the months before the United States entered World War II, Congress passed the Smith Act of 1940, which made it illegal "to knowingly or willfully advocate, abet, advise, or teach the duty, necessity, desirability, or propriety of overthrowing" the United States government by force.[43] The Second Red Scare of the late 1940s and early 1950s— embodied in Senator Joseph McCarthy's destructive witch hunts against real and imagined communists and communist sympathizers—led to the Internal Security Act of 1950. This law required communist organizations to register with the Justice Department and established a Subversive Activities Control Board to investigate people suspected of promoting "totalitarian dictatorship."

In the 1951 case of *Dennis v. United States*, decided during the height of McCarthyism, a divided Supreme Court sustained the main anti-communist measures of the 1940s and 1950s.[44] Eugene Dennis was the general secretary of the American Communist Party. In 1948, he and ten other party leaders were indicted for violating the Smith Act of 1940. They were not charged with directly conspiring to overthrow the government but rather with conspiracy to organize "a society, group, and assembly of persons who teach and advocate the overthrow and destruction of the Government of the United States by force and violence." Dennis and nine of his peers were sentenced to five years in prison, and by a 7–2 vote the justices ruled that their conviction was constitutional.[45]

Not until after McCarthy's downfall did the justices reextend protections for political dissenters. In *Yates v. United States* (1957), the Court held that a person could not be prosecuted for "advocacy and teaching of forcible overthrow as an abstract principle, divorced from any effort to instigate action to that end."[46] Justice Hugo Black's concurring opinion reiterated the logic of extending broad protections to speech:

> Doubtlessly, dictators have to stamp out causes and beliefs which they deem subversive to their evil regimes. But government suppression of causes and beliefs seems to be the very antithesis of what our Constitution stands for. . . . The

First Amendment provides the only kind of security system that can preserve a free government—one that leaves the way open for people to favor, discuss, advocate, or incite causes and doctrines however obnoxious and antagonistic such views may be to the rest of us.[47]

In the 1950s and 1960s, the most important beneficiaries of newly expanded free speech protections were participants in the civil rights movement. The messages of civil rights protestors were considered deeply offensive, harmful, and dangerous to many southern government officials, and citizens considered the ideas of civil rights protestors "subversive" to southern life in the same way that communist and anarchist ideas were considered subversive to the country as a whole. In fact, much of the language used against protestors minimized their actual concern about civil rights and attempted instead to associate movement leaders with radical, destructive elements in society. J. Edgar Hoover's FBI tried to link Martin Luther King Jr. and other civil rights leaders to communism.[48] Under any standard that allowed the government to censor or punish speech that was offensive or had a tendency to cause harm or danger, the civil rights movement could not have gotten off the ground.

Civil rights leaders were able to maintain the movement because the federal courts were willing to apply stronger free speech principles to stop southern governments from repressing protestors. Many southern political leaders tried vigorously to suppress African American protests by forcing the NAACP to identify its members (so that they could then be targeted for harassment or worse),[49] forbidding NAACP lawyers from soliciting clients for cases attacking the constitutionality of racial segregation,[50] charging protestors with disturbing the peace,[51] suing civil rights leaders for libeling pro-segregationist community leaders,[52] and limiting speakers' access to public property.[53] The Supreme Court declared all these measures unconstitutional. Given that much of the movement's political strategy depended on exposing repressive southern practices to northern opinion, the free flow of information was fundamental to the movement's success. The extension of First Amendment protections allowed Martin Luther King Jr. and other civil rights leaders to build the national support needed to pass such laws as the Civil Rights Act of 1964 and the Voting Rights Act of 1965.

The Supreme Court was also remarkably protective of speech during the Vietnam War. Although the justices did not extend free speech protection to the act of burning a draft card,[54] there was no repeat of the prosecutions of anti-war speech that occurred during World War I. Presidential candidate Eugene McCarthy made the same kinds of statements in 1968 that got presidential candidate Eugene Debs sentenced to prison after he expressed them in 1920.

By the late 1960s the Supreme Court had formally adopted the views of "Holmes and Brandeis in dissent" as the new constitutional standard for evaluating government's authority to censor or punish speakers whose words might be considered a threat to public order, safety, or morality. In *Brandenburg v. Ohio* (1969), the Court overturned the conviction of a Ku Klux Klan member who said during a speech that "if our President, our Congress, our Supreme Court, continues to suppress the white, Caucasian race, it's possible that there might have to be some revengeance [*sic*] taken."[55] The

justices ruled that the government cannot "forbid or proscribe advocacy of the use of force or of law violation except
where such advocacy is directed to inciting or producing
imminent lawless action and is likely to incite or produce
such action."[56] And to finally bury the older way of thinking,
the justices held: "The contrary teaching of *Whitney v.
California* . . . cannot be supported, and that decision is therefore overturned."[57]

Two years later, California prosecuted nineteen-year-old
Paul Robert Cohen for disturbing the peace in the corridor of
a courthouse by wearing a jacket bearing the words "Fuck the
Draft."[58] In *Cohen v. California* (1971) the justices overturned
his conviction, asserting that it was not within the power of
government to "remove this offensive word from the public
vocabulary."[59] Justice John Marshall Harlan acknowledged
that this ruling would create a marketplace of ideas that included "verbal tumult, discord, and even offensive utterance,"
but these were "necessary side effects of the broader enduring
values which the process of open debate permits us to
achieve."[60] He added, "one man's vulgarity is another's lyric."[61]

The Court's embrace of free speech had other beneficiaries. Historically, people who spoke out against religion could
be convicted of "blasphemy," but in 1952 the justices in *Joseph
Burstyn, Inc. v. Wilson* ruled that "it is not the business of government in our nation to suppress real or imagined attacks
upon a particular religious doctrine."[62] In 1957, copies of Allen
Ginsberg's poem "Howl" were seized by customs officials,
and a San Francisco bookstore manager was arrested for sell-
ing a published copy to an undercover police officer; this
would not happen again after the free speech revolution of

the 1960s. (The 2010 film *Howl*, starring James Franco, dramatizes the subsequent trial.) Counterculture celebrities such as the comedian and social critic Lenny Bruce, who was arrested in the early 1960s for using the word "schmuck" (a Yiddish word for penis), eventually benefited from the Court's willingness to accommodate "even offensive utterances" that posed no immediate danger of violence or lawlessness.[63] While obscenity law is not entirely a thing of the past,[64] the contemporary legal and cultural environment is tremendously accommodating of forms of expression that would have landed many people in jail in the era of the Comstock Act.

If today we take for granted that the government cannot put people in jail for asserting "countercultural" attitudes or identities—including forms of expression that challenge traditional religion, prevailing social mores, familiar lifestyle choices, inherited views about sexuality, or historic gender roles—then it is good to keep in mind that this was made possible by the twentieth-century revolution in free speech rights.

The expansion of free speech protection does not prevent the law from addressing many of the harms that can result from speech acts. A person can be censored or punished for revealing national security secrets. A person can be held liable for speech that is an invasion of privacy. There are also narrowly drawn categories of speech that the law treats as unprotected, including incitement of illegal activity, defamation, fighting words, true threats, harassment, and speech that creates an unsafe or discriminatory working or learning environment. Still, all of these categories are bounded in a way that ensures they cannot be used to censor or punish people just for expressing ideas.

Many of today's advocates for censorship believe that denying free speech is a way of protecting vulnerable groups. But social progress has come about not as a result of silencing certain speakers, but by ensuring that previously silenced or marginalized groups are empowered to find their voice and have their say. Our country became better, more just, and more inclusive in the twentieth century in part because of the contributions of expanded protections for free speech. That is why sturdy protection for the expression of ideas should be considered one of the past century's most important accomplishments.

THE LESSONS OF HISTORY

Each generation brings new calls to suppress speech, for reasons that appear noble at the time. Today it is to help create inclusive learning environments for students, and also to stop speech that might help terrorists. Not long ago, it was to stop pornography on the ground that it was discrimination against women. From the 1920s until the 1960s, it was to stop communism. During World War I, it was to preserve the draft and win the war. The specific issues vary, but the underlying question is always the same: when to stop speech that is perceived as harmful. One of the key lessons of history is that almost always, on reflection, society concludes these efforts were misguided. As Justice Holmes put it, "time has upset many fighting faiths."[65]

We cannot think clearly about free speech on campuses today unless we understand this history of freedom of expression. As we continue to debate this issue, it is vital that participants appreciate the rise of a free speech tradition as a truly historic accomplishment. And as important as free speech is to society as a whole, there are additional reasons why it deserves an even higher degree of protection within institutions of higher education.

CHAPTER THREE

Nullius in Verba: *Free Speech at Colleges and Universities*

ISTORICALLY, governments and societies have not been organized around democracy and free choice, but around fixed ideas of who should rule and how people should behave. The vast majority of people have enjoyed very little freedom to think or express themselves in ways that challenged prevailing authority and prevailing opinion.

Similarly, for many centuries, higher education was not founded on free thought but on indoctrination. Medieval universities established in Europe between the eleventh and fourteenth centuries were grounded in Christian traditions and were organized much like the advanced madrassas of Islamic Spain and the Emirate of Sicily. The flow of ideas was limited to the accepted range of theological discussion among believers, supplemented by Latin, mathematics, biblical astronomy and physics, moral philosophy, and classical grammar, logic, and rhetoric. The curriculum consisted of some Aristotle and some Cicero (and related thinkers), but it was mostly the New Testament, just as the Quran was the main text in advanced educational institutions in Islamic Europe and the Middle East.[1]

This was the system faced by Galileo when he challenged the prevailing orthodoxy that the earth was the center of the universe. His suggestion that the earth and the planets revolved around the sun was denounced by some church authorities as "foolish and absurd in philosophy, and formally heretical since it explicitly contradicts in many places the sense of Holy Scripture."[2] As happens in systems dedicated to the promotion of an assumed orthodoxy, Galileo received explicit instructions from Pope Paul V "to abandon completely . . . the opinion that the sun still stands at the center of the world and the earth moves, and henceforth not to hold, teach, or defend it in any way whatever, either orally or in writing."[3]

If we still thought that the purpose of higher education was indoctrination, there would be no need for freedom of thought and speech. If one starts from an assumption of already knowing the truth—religious, political, or otherwise—then higher education is merely about instructing students to become disciples. We see such a thing today in the higher education systems of theocratic and authoritarian regimes.

To imagine a special role for freedom of thought and speech one must imagine a university that is designed to serve some purpose other than indoctrination. What could that purpose be?

Rather than create disciples who will preserve some unchanging wisdom, institutions of higher education might dedicate themselves to the creation of disciplined free thinkers who seek new knowledge and are willing to challenge received wisdom if that's where facts and reason take them. Such a community would value expert training and rigorous thinking, but it would also value curiosity, discovery, skepticism, and dissenting viewpoints. Ideas that seemed wrong would not be censored or shouted down but engaged and exposed through argumentation. People who advocated such ideas with rigor and expertise would not be ignored or denied a chance to be heard; rather, they would be permitted, and even encouraged, to challenge authorities with whom they disagreed.

In the modern western tradition, the belief in the value of such a university began to take shape, tentatively, in the seventeenth century, around the time that John Milton began to argue in favor of the toleration of dissenting opinion. The model of such an institution was not traditional monasteries and madrassas, but rather the attitude adopted by members of the Royal Society of London for Improving Natural Knowledge.

Established in 1663, the Royal Society took as its motto the Latin phrase *Nullius in verba*, which can be translated as "take nobody's word for it" or "nobody tells us how to think."[4] The members of the Royal Society were bound by the view that one should not hold a belief merely because someone in authority demanded agreement with it. Rather, beliefs should be tested by free-thinking human beings, and those free-thinking people would decide for themselves what was true after engaging in debate and experimentation. This was especially vital for any group of people who dedicated themselves to the creation and transmission of knowledge. Without such a rule, it is hard to imagine the creation of knowledge at all, since there is almost always some existing explanation for any phenomenon, generally with authoritative backing.

This view of human reason and rational inquiry enabled the Royal Society to nurture the scientific revolution by publishing Isaac Newton's *Principia Mathematica*,[5] providing the first English account of inoculation, and helping Benjamin Franklin tell the people of the world that any one of them could discover for themselves the electrical nature of lightning simply by using a kite and a key.[6]

Among all the inventions of modern life, few have been more important for promoting human freedom and social progress than the university, organized around the search for knowledge based on free inquiry and debate rooted in reason and experimentation.

Such a thing did not come easily in the United States. In order to have a perspective on contemporary debates about the scope of freedom to express controversial views on campuses, it is important to look at the history of American higher education. As with the history of free speech, the record shows that restrictions on freedom of thought and expression on campuses have been used to stifle and punish dissenters, social critics, vulnerable and marginalized voices, and the sort of innovative thinkers who fuel social progress. The history shows that campuses cannot censor or punish the expression of ideas, or allow intimidation or disruption of those who are expressing ideas, without undermining their core function of promoting inquiry, discovery, and the dissemination of new knowledge. Although the protections of the First Amendment apply only to America's public colleges and universities (which are government entities), the principles of inquiry and academic freedom we describe should be the same at every institution of higher education, public or private.

In this chapter we begin with a short history of higher education in the United States, sketching the transformation of colleges from places of religious instruction to institutions that value and protect rigorous free inquiry. We then examine the importance within colleges and universities not just of free speech but of a culture of scholarly inquiry, where norms of academic freedom are linked to expectations of professionalism, and where there is tolerance of dissenting and even offensive viewpoints. Next we examine the Berkeley Free Speech Movement, which established an expectation that campuses extend full First Amendment protections to personal and political speech outside the professional and civil settings of the classroom.

FROM DISCIPLES TO DISCIPLINED FREE THINKERS

Early American denominational colleges were founded on evangelical fervor and emphasized Christian piety over Enlightenment rationalism. There was little room for dissenting opinion. New colonies and new colleges often formed because individuals were essentially banished from existing settlements and campuses. Theological battles at Harvard played a role in the founding of Yale College in 1701.[7] Later, splits among factions at Yale led some exiles to found Dartmouth College in 1769.[8] When Roger Williams was forced out by Massachusetts Bay theocrats over issues of religious liberty, he helped found Rhode Island and, in 1765, Brown University.[9] In the words of historian Walter P. Metzger, the early American college "was centered in tradition, . . . looked to antiquity for the tools of thought, to Christianity for the by-laws of living; it supplied furniture and discipline for the mind, but constrained intellectual adventure."[10]

By the early nineteenth century, some American educators were traveling to European universities and returning with a newfound respect for free inquiry. George Ticknor, a historian at Harvard who received an advanced education at the University of Göttingen in Germany, reported that at German universities the enthusiasm for genuine learning resulted in "an universal toleration in all matters of opinion. . . . No matter what a man thinks, he may teach it and print it, not only without molestation from the government but also without molestation from publick opinion which is so often more oppressive than the aim of authority."[11] When the young Henry Wadsworth Longfellow was a student at Göttingen in 1829, he contrasted the American idea of a university, which he described as "two or three large brick buildings,—with a chapel, and a President to pray in it!" with the German idea "of collecting together professors in whom the spirit moved— who were well enough known to attract students to themselves, and . . . capable of teaching them something they did not know before."[12] Late in his life, Thomas Jefferson could write that the "new university" he was helping to create "will be based on the illimitable freedom of the human mind[,] for here we are not afraid to follow truth wherever it may lead, nor to tolerate any error so long as reason is left free to combat it."[13]

But as with free speech in the United States, the transition from valuing orthodoxy to valuing freedom of thought and expression did not really gain steam until the late nineteenth and early twentieth centuries. Initially, the major driver behind the transition was the development of scientific ideas that called into question some tenets of Christian orthodoxy. The most important examples were the publications of Charles Lyell's three-volume *Principles of Geology* (1830–33),[14] which challenged biblical accounts of the age of the planet and the origins of life on earth, and Darwin's *Origin of Species*[15] in 1859, with its earth-shaking conclusions about the evolutionary origins of humankind.

The development of scientific findings that contested Christian teachings led to equal and opposite reactions: a theocratic backlash, and increased advocacy for separating the pursuit of knowledge from its evangelical origins. As for the former, it should be no surprise that the more the college's self-image was linked to Christian theology, the less willing it was to accept views that challenged that theology. The presidents of the religiously oriented Amherst College, Williams College, Hamilton College, and Lafayette College prohibited the teaching of Darwin at their schools for decades. Vanderbilt, which in 1873 had been converted from a school for the training of ministers to a multipurpose university, was still in the grip of its Christian heritage when it dismissed a faculty member for suggesting the pre-Adamite origins of humans.[16]

But in the decades after the Civil War, a new development in American higher education was occurring that drew inspiration from the early example of Galileo, the antiauthoritarian creed of the Royal Society, the impressive contributions of science over the previous century, the midcentury Emersonian celebration of the free-thinking person in America, and the recent creation of the National Academy of Science. It was reflected not only in a gradual waning of the sectarian character of established institutions such as Yale, Princeton, and Harvard, but also the founding between 1865 and 1890 of Johns Hopkins, Stanford, Chicago, and public and land-grant universities such as Cornell and the University of California. Each of these was explicitly nonsectarian and inspired by the German example. At such institutions, a topic such as evolution "was not gall and wormwood, but everyday nourishing fare."[17]

For American universities to become centers of rigorous inquiry, decisions about what ideas could be taught or expressed had to be taken out of the hands of boards, administrators, politicians, and donors and given to an expertly trained, independent faculty. The most important leaders who worked to ensure the autonomy of faculty in matters of inquiry were Andrew Dickson White (Cornell's president from 1866 to 1885), Daniel Coit Gilman (who became the third president of the University of California in 1872 and the first president of Johns Hopkins in 1875), Charles William Eliot (the president of Harvard from 1869 to 1909), and William Rainey Harper (who became the first president of the University of Chicago in 1891).[18]

White, who had studied at the University of Berlin in the 1850s (while traveling with his former Yale classmate Daniel

Gilman), spent decades promoting the separation of universities from religious sectarianism and arguing that science, not religion, was the key to human freedom.[19] At the University of California, Gilman advocated language training in German and French so that American scholars could "keep abreast of the progress of discovery in Berlin, Vienna, and Paris." Unlike the University of Illinois (which opened in 1868) and the University of Michigan (founded decades earlier), Gilman's University of California was not a Christian university. He never spoke of it in those terms, and there were no mandatory worship services or presidential lectures on Christian topics. (During his tenure, it did not even have a voluntary chapel, making it perhaps the most secular college in America at the time.)[20] When he moved to the new Johns Hopkins University and addressed the trustees on January 30, 1875, he asserted:

> The Institution we are about to organize would not be worthy the name of a university, if it were to be devoted to any other purpose than the discovery and promulgation of the truth; and it would be ignoble in the extreme if the resources which have been given by the founder without restrictions should be limited to the maintenance of ecclesiastical differences or perverted to the promotion of political strife.
>
> As the spirit of the University should be that of intellectual freedom in pursuit of the truth and of the broadest charity toward those from whom we differ in opinion it is certain that sectarian and partisan preferences should have no control in the selection of teachers, and should not be apparent in the official work.[21]

Gilman's comments anticipated the other major obstacle to the university's protection of the full range of beliefs: external pressures for political conformity. Like those fighting the larger battle over free speech protections generally, the leaders of American higher education in the late nineteenth century had to find their way toward freedom of thought in relation to politics.

The same fears of anarchism, labor unrest, and eastern European immigration that triggered late nineteenth-century political repression were also felt on college campuses. Some university leaders took steps to fortify freedom of thought; others did not. In the 1890s, when University of Wisconsin economics professor Richard Ely was attacked by state politicians because of his support for labor rights, the university's faculty rallied to his defense, prompting their regents to declare that "Whatever may be the limitations which trammel inquiry elsewhere we believe the great state University of Wisconsin should ever encourage the continual and fearless sifting and winnowing by which alone the truth can be found"—a statement that is now proudly memorialized as "the Wisconsin Idea."[22] By contrast, when Jane Stanford, benefactor and co-founder of Stanford University, judged professor Edward Ross in 1900 to be unacceptably radical because of his support for unions and the Free Silver political movement, she forced his firing, leading to many faculty resignations and a reputation for political censorship that hampered the university's development for decades.[23]

Closely watching the events at Stanford was William Rainey Harper, the first president of the University of Chicago. Harper was determined to make sure the Stanford experience would not be reproduced at his new university. Two years after the Ross affair, during the decennial of the University of Chicago, Harper asserted a creed that has remained fundamental to the identity of that university:

the principle of complete freedom of speech on all subjects has from the beginning been regarded as fundamental in the University of Chicago [and] this principle can neither now nor at any future time be called into question. . . . Freedom of expression must be given to members of a university faculty, even though it be abused; for, as has been said, the abuse of it is not so great an evil as the restriction of such liberty.[24]

This perspective was woven so firmly into the culture of the university that when, in the 1930s, a student organization invited Communist Party candidate William Z. Foster to campus and triggered demands for punishment and censorship, President Robert M. Hutchins responded that "our students . . . should have freedom to discuss any problem that presents itself," and (echoing Holmes and Brandeis) that the "cure" for ideas we oppose "lies through open discussion rather than through inhibition."[25] Later Hutchins would say, "free inquiry is indispensable to the good life, that universities exist for the sake of such inquiry, [and] without it they cease to be universities."[26]

Such views did not receive widespread support in the early twentieth century. The American Association of University Professors (AAUP) was founded in January 1915 in direct response to a wave of threats against the freedom of the faculty to hold and express unpopular views.[27] The public was still hostile to the idea that universities should nurture free inquiry. One historian summarizes the accumulating threats this way:

Distress signals came from the University of Utah, where seventeen professors resigned in protest when four of their colleagues were unceremoniously removed; from the University of Colorado, where a law professor believed he had been fired for testimony given before a government commission; from Wesleyan University, where a professor believed he had been removed because of anti-Sabbatarian remarks delivered at a nearby café; from the University of Pennsylvania, where Scott Nearing, in a case that achieved great notoriety, was removed from the Wharton School; from the University of Washington, where three professors had been discharged.[28]

The AAUP's founding president was the great American philosopher John Dewey, a product of Johns Hopkins (where he received his doctorate in 1884) and the University of Chicago (where he was a faculty member from 1894 to 1904).[29] As America's leading philosopher of democracy and its relationship to experimental thinking, Dewey was well positioned to defend the idea of academic freedom. As he once put it, "Since freedom of mind and freedom of expression are the root of all freedom, to deny freedom in education is a crime against democracy."[30] By December 1915 the AAUP was prepared to publish its "Declaration of Principles on Academic Freedom and Academic Tenure," which emphasized the importance not only of scientific advancements but also of allowing a broader range of opinion on matters of public interest than might be tolerated in society at large:

> Public opinion is at once the chief safeguard of a democracy, and the chief menace to the real liberty of the individual. . . . An inviolable refuge from such tyranny should be found in the university. It should be an intellectual experiment station, where new ideas may germinate and where their fruit, though still distasteful to the community as a whole, may be allowed to ripen until finally, perchance, it may become a part of the accepted intellectual food of the nation or of the world. . . . One of its most characteristic functions in a democratic society is to help make public opinion more self-critical and

more circumspect, to check the more hasty and unconsidered impulses of popular feeling, to train the democracy to the habit of looking before and after.[31]

This statement set in motion a decades-long effort to protect faculty members from being punished merely because their views were considered wrongheaded or harmful. As it was for free speech rights generally, the Cold War was a bad time for dissenters in higher education. In the early 1940s, the city college system of New York and the University of California decided that membership in the Communist Party disqualified a person from being on their faculties. The California Regents explained its reasoning this way: "The Communist Party . . . gives its first loyalty to a foreign political movement and, perhaps, to a foreign government" rather than to the scholar's professional obligation of candor and objectivity.[32] In 1948, a state Un-American Activities Committee looked into alleged communist activities at the University of Washington, causing a number of alleged communist professors to be fired over the objections of a faculty tenure committee. The presidents of Harvard and Yale announced that they would not hire communists on their faculties, with Yale president Charles Seymour clarifying, "There will be no witch-hunts at Yale, because there will be no witches."[33]

By the 1950s the bans and firings extended from "card-carrying" Communists (who acknowledged their current or past affiliation) to "Fifth Amendment" communists, who were punished for refusing to answer questions about their political views. In 1956, the presidents of the nation's thirty-seven leading universities, under the auspices of the Association of American Universities, drew up a statement declaring that a professor's unwillingness to answer questions about his affiliations "cannot fail to reflect upon a profession that claims for itself the fullest freedom to speak and the maximum protection of that freedom in our society," and thus raised serious questions about that person's fitness to hold a faculty position.[34] The climate was so repressive that even the AAUP did not speak out against anti-communist policies at the time.[35]

By the late 1960s, however, widespread support for the civil rights movement and widespread opposition to the Vietnam War had given the toleration of political dissent a firm foothold in the academy. The act of challenging government policies and academic orthodoxies came to be seen as a force for progress rather than a sign of professional irresponsibility. Professors did not lose their jobs for speaking out against the Vietnam War, and eminent ones did speak out. Scholarship that questioned prevailing attitudes about economic justice, environmental sustainability, historical consciousness, race and ethnicity, women's rights, and gender relations benefited from expanded notions of academic freedom.[36]

We acknowledge that we have framed the fight for free thinking in higher education as a rather stark choice: institutions of higher education can either protect an orthodoxy against challenge or be willing to permit all ideas; they can either treat students as disciples or help them become disciplined independent thinkers. Either there is complete protection for the expression of all ideas and views, or there is an orthodoxy of belief.

One might hope for a middle ground. Are we really limited to choosing between the absence of free thinking and a completely unregulated marketplace of ideas?

We believe there is no middle ground. History demonstrates that there is no way to define an unacceptable, punishment-worthy idea without putting genuinely important new thinking and societal critique at risk. Universities contribute to society when faculty are allowed to explore the frontiers of knowledge and suggest ways of thinking that may be considered crazy, distasteful, or offensive to the community. When people ask the censor to suppress bad ideas in higher education, many important and positive ideas never have the chance to flourish, and many dangerous or evil ideas are allowed to thrive because they are not subjected to evaluation, critique, and rebuttal. In our view, no belief should be treated as sacrosanct. *Nullius in verba* remains vital: we must be willing to subject all ideas to the test.

As a final example, consider what happened in the mid-1990s when the psychologist Richard J. Herrnstein and the political scientist Charles Murray published their book *The Bell Curve: Intelligence and Class Structure in American Life*.[37] They advanced the extremely controversial thesis that there were racial differences in intelligence and that these differences are important factors influencing economic and social success in the United States. Many critics found deeply offensive the idea that blacks in America were overall less successful than whites not because of persistent discrimination, but because they were less intelligent.

Although it would have been tempting to prevent such an idea from being expressed at all, the ability of academic experts to engage and criticize the analysis proved much more important.[38] Popular commentators, lacking the expertise to scrutinize the authors' statistical analyses, were impressed by the appearance of rigor. Scholars, however, noted that the authors' claimed measurement of intelligence actually also measured education, which fundamentally undermined their claims about proving the effects of inherent intelligence. Most public commentators did not focus on one passing footnote, where Herrnstein and Murray indicated a higher correlation between a college degree and family income than between IQ and family income, thus opening up a more standard argument about the importance of educational opportunity. The authors claimed that the genetic component of IQ might be as high as 80 percent, but when experts at Carnegie Mellon reexamined the basis of their claim, they found the actual number was between 34 and 46 percent.[39] The American Psychological Association's Board of Scientific Affairs found that there is zero evidence supporting the claim that differences in IQ test scores between whites and blacks are due to genetics rather than many other alternative hypotheses (including caste and culture).[40] William J. Matthews and Stephen Jay Gould argued that the authors' entire argument was premised on four dubious assumptions: intelligence must be reducible to a single number, it must be possible to rank people by intelligence in linear order, intelligence must be primarily genetically based, and intelligence must be essentially immutable.[41]

More could be said; the scholarly assessments of the book are voluminous.[42] The example illustrates our basic point: rather than being worse off because such an argument was allowed to circulate, society was much better off because others had an opportunity to subject the book to the highest standards of academic scholarship and provide compelling refutation of its methodology and conclusions.

FOSTERING A CULTURE OF
UNFETTERED INQUIRY

Modern colleges and universities achieved their present respect and importance only when they fully embraced a culture of unfettered scholarly inquiry. That culture has two central components: establishing and maintaining norms of academic freedom that acknowledge the faculty's professional obligations, and nurturing a spirit of tolerance within the broader campus community that allows all ideas to be subjected to debate and assessment.

The AAUP's historic 1915 Declaration emphasized professors' right to express themselves "to students and to the general public, without fear or favor."[43] But it also expressed the view that the results of their inquiries "be set forth with dignity, courtesy, and temperateness of language."[44] The "pledge" of the AAUP was "not only that the profession will earnestly guard those liberties without which it cannot rightly render its distinctive and indispensable service to society, but also that it will with equal earnestness seek to maintain such standards of professional character, and of scientific integrity and competence, as shall make it a fit instrument for that service."[45]

From the beginning, therefore, the commitment to academic freedom was inextricably linked to commitment to nurturing and enforcing the norms of an expert, professional, scholarly community. Whether a photon is a wave or a particle or something else is to be resolved not by having faculty members disrupt and censor those who advocate different views, but by coming up with better ideas, arguments, and experiments.

Once we appreciate that, within the realm of professional academic freedom, the notion that "all ideas are protected" is linked to the notion of "maintaining standards of professional character," we can see that colleges and universities actually must impose extensive regulation on speech *in professional settings*. A partial list of how colleges and universities regulate speech in these settings would include the following:

- Campus faculties and administrators may limit the topics that can be discussed in classrooms to those related to the topic of the course, even though this sort of subject-matter restriction would not be acceptable if states or localities attempted to limit what people can say in their everyday lives.

- Campus faculties and administrators may expect teachers and students to treat each other with professionalism and mutual respect in an educational setting. Abusive or profane language that would be protected in society in general can be prohibited in educational spaces on campus.

- Campus faculties and administrators may make judgments about the quality of professors' or students' work based on the content of what is said— meaning that students can be given better or worse grades, and professors can be granted or denied promotion and tenure, as long as the evaluative standards are linked to matters of professional judgment and standards of quality rather than discriminatory considerations (such as a person's partisanship or ideology, or the views that he or she express more broadly in public settings).

At universities, a biology department may choose not to hire a creationist on the grounds that the person lacks professional competence, although they may not discriminate against a Republican. A history department may choose not to hire a person who denies the Holocaust in the Third Reich on the grounds that the person lacks professional competence, but it cannot refuse to hire a candidate whose work is otherwise excellent because they learn that he or she is a member of a neo-Nazi party. Resources to support innovative scholarship can be given to scholars whose work is considered by other scholars to be of high quality and promising (a content-based decision), but it cannot be withdrawn because decision makers disagree with the applicant's Facebook postings. A university can fire the head of an admissions committee who made derogatory comments about Jewish applicants, and can take actions against professors who never allow students to express conservative views in class, because in each case professional norms are being violated.

As Cass R. Sunstein writes, "The university can impose subject-matter or other restrictions on speech only to the extent that the restrictions are closely related to its educational mission."[46] The point is articulated this way in the Academic Policy Manual of the University of California (APM 010):

> [Principles of academic freedom] reflect the University's fundamental mission, which is to discover knowledge and to disseminate it to its students and to society at large. . . . The University also seeks to foster in its students a mature independence of mind, and this purpose cannot be achieved

unless students and faculty are free within the classroom to express the widest range of viewpoints in accord with the standards of scholarly inquiry and professional ethics. The exercise of academic freedom entails correlative duties of professional care when teaching, conducting research, or otherwise acting as a member of the faculty. . . . Academic freedom requires that teaching and scholarship be assessed by reference to the professional standards that sustain the University's pursuit and achievement of knowledge. The substance and nature of these standards properly lie within the expertise and authority of the faculty as a body.[47]

With respect to students' rights within academic settings—what APM 010 refers to as "student freedom of scholarly inquiry"—the faculty is expected to ensure that students are allowed to critically examine course material and be judged in accordance with fair procedures solely on the basis of their academic performance, and not on whether the professor agrees with a student's personal views.[48] Moreover,

No student can abridge the rights of other students when exercising their right to differ. Students should be free to take civil and reasoned exception to the data or views offered in any course of study and to reserve judgment about matters of opinion, but they are responsible for learning the content of any course of study [and the] faculty has authority for all aspects of the course, including content, structure, relevance of alternative points of view, and evaluations.[49]

There will always be disagreements over whether a particular statement by a faculty member while acting in a professional capacity should be considered within the standards of scholarly inquiry and professional ethics, or what constitutes unprofessional or disruptive behavior at faculty meetings or academic conferences, or what statements or behaviors by students in instructional or research settings are inconsistent with the purposes of those settings. Still, a university's punishment of a faculty member or student never can be based merely on an objection to a stated idea. Rather, it requires an independent, fact-based assessment of the impact particular statements or behaviors have on the person's professional fitness and the university's scholarly mission.[50]

There is always a risk that the scholarly evaluation of the "quality" of work can be influenced by ideology rather than objective measures, and these influences can be subtle. It is, of course, wrong for law schools to refuse to hire someone who has conservative rather than liberal views. But it is not at all uncommon for faculty members to have a higher regard for views with which they are already sympathetic. University leaders and faculties need to be relentless about ensuring that scholarly quality is not just a cover for ideological agreement, and that there is ongoing appreciation for how diversity of perspective mitigates the errors of groupthink and contributes to the mission of inquiry and discovery.[51] More generally, the integrity of the enterprise presupposes the existence of meaningful standards of quality and professional conduct that can guide decision making within the academy.

Although academic freedom and standards of professional conduct are crucial in formal educational settings, they are not by themselves enough to ensure the maintenance of a culture of scholarly inquiry. That requires a second component as well: a willingness within the broader campus community to embrace and defend the unfettered exchange of ideas.

Free speech and academic freedom can be undermined not only by official censorship and punishment but also by members of the academic community who are intolerant of ideas with which they disagree. Even in institutions dedicated to advancing truth and questioning past assumptions, the pressure to conform to dominant opinion is an ever-present threat. The history of science—to take just one area—is littered with people who risked their careers to promote absurd and heretical ideas that later turned out to be true. Tolerance of views considered wrongheaded or dangerous is not a natural condition anywhere. The success of academic communities depends as much on continually reinvigorating this sentiment than on establishing formal protections for academic freedom. This point echoes a view expressed by Albert Einstein, who wrote:

> Laws alone cannot secure freedom of expression; in order that every man present his views without penalty there must be a spirit of tolerance in the entire population. Such an ideal of external liberty can never be fully attained but must be sought unremittingly if scientific thought, and philosophical and creative thinking in general, are to be advanced as far as possible.[52]

As we have seen all too often, a failure to achieve a spirit of tolerance on campuses can take a number of forms, including refusals to allow student groups to invite controversial speakers to campus,[53] protests designed to prevent controversial individuals from speaking,[54] demands that campus newspapers be defunded or that newspaper editors resign after publishing a controversial op-ed,[55] requirements for "trigger warnings" on course materials that some consider objectionable or potentially upsetting,[56] efforts to prevent students from expressing relevant but dissenting views in class, and calls to dismiss faculty members from administrative positions if they express views contrary to those held by certain campus groups.[57]

Although it is consistent with free speech values for students and others to express their disagreement or outrage at controversial speakers or objectionable views, we have seen too many cases where the energy was directed at silencing others instead of rebutting them. Rather than view campuses as places that must provide special protections for unfettered inquiry, some students and faculty view them as privileged arenas for the expression of respectable ideas. They consequently argue that university leaders should provide "no platform" for ideas considered unworthy.

The "no platform" policy originated in a decision by the UK National Union of Students (NUS) in 1974 to ensure that certain proscribed persons and organizations be denied any venue to speak on campuses.[58] According to the NUS policy, no "individuals or members of organisations or groups identified by the Democratic Procedures Committee as holding racist or fascist views" may attend or speak at any NUS function or conference.[59] The organization then creates a blacklist of speakers and organizations and also insists that no NUS member share a platform with anyone on the blacklist. In a 2016 poll, nearly two-thirds of university students in the UK approved of such policies.[60]

Originally reserved for fascist parties such as the British National Party, the no-platform blacklist has been used more recently to prevent campus appearances of feminist writer Germaine Greer, human rights activist Maryam Namazie, and HOPE not Hate founder Nick Lowles, out of fear that some students would find their opinions upsetting. This denial of a platform for controversial speakers stems from the NUS claim that universities should "balance freedom of speech and freedom from harm" in order to accommodate "safer space activism."[61]

There is a place at colleges and universities for the concept of "safe spaces." We have already seen that, in settings such as classrooms or department meetings, it is necessary to create an environment of civility and mutual respect, in order to facilitate the expression of the widest range of viewpoints in accord with the standards of scholarly inquiry and professional ethics. Students are also free to self-organize in ways that reflect shared interests and allow them to talk about their experiences without always needing to defend themselves.[62] But the "safer space activism" of the no-platform movement is not motivated by a desire to create the conditions whereby members of the academic community feel safe to express their views. It is also not motivated by a desire to prevent physical harm, harassment, intimidation, or any of the limited categories of speech that provide a basis for punishment. Rather, the premise is that the academic community should be a safe space for those who consider themselves harmed when they are exposed to views with which they disagree.[63]

Accepting this as a legitimate premise for censorship undermines all protections for dissenting or even disagreeable speech, and is therefore not a kind of harm that universities should try to prevent and not the kind of safe space that universities can establish. More important, the idea of "no platform" itself reflects a misunderstanding of universities. They are not arenas reserved for high-minded and approved ways of thinking. They are spaces where all ideas can be expressed and challenged. The platform that campuses provide is designed to be an open platform, not one reserved for those who are thinking correct thoughts.

This no-platform mindset also motivates some students in the United States to demand that universities sanction people for writing "I'm with Trump" or "Build That Wall" in chalk on college campuses,[64] to force university administrators to cancel an appearance by the conservative writer Ben Shapiro (who was to speak on how diversity initiatives can hamper free speech),[65] to demand the resignation of a student leader who posted an "All Lives Matter" Twitter message in the wake of the assassination of five police officers in Dallas,[66] or to demand a federal investigation after professor Laura Kipnis wrote a scholarly essay questioning campus attitudes about sexual relations.[67] The list, which is almost endless, demonstrates conclusively one simple lesson: advocating the censorship or punishment of harmful or offensive speech inevitably leads groups to try to silence people merely because they have different beliefs.

Concerns about a culture of intolerance on college campuses led President Obama to tell Rutgers graduates in 2016 that democracy and education require a willingness to listen to people with whom you disagree:

> I know a couple years ago, folks on this campus got upset that Condoleezza Rice was supposed to speak at a commencement. Now, I don't think it's a secret that I disagree with many of the foreign policies of Dr. Rice and the previous administration. But the notion that this community or country would be better served by not hearing from a former Secretary of State, or shutting out what she had to say—I believe that's misguided. . . .

If you disagree with somebody, bring them in and ask them tough questions. Hold their feet to the fire. Make them defend their positions. If somebody has got a bad or offensive idea, prove it wrong. Engage it. Debate it. Stand up for what you believe in. Don't be scared to take somebody on. Don't feel like you got to shut your ears off because you're too fragile and somebody might offend your sensibilities. Go at them if they're not making any sense. Use your logic and reason and words. And by doing so, you'll strengthen your own position, and you'll hone your arguments. And maybe you'll learn something and realize you don't know everything. And you may have a new understanding not only about what your opponents believe but maybe what you believe. Either way, you win. And more importantly, our democracy wins.[68]

In the words of University of California president Clark Kerr, "The University is not engaged in making ideas safe for students. It is engaged in making students safe for ideas."[69] There are plenty of ways a young person can avoid exposure to new or challenging ideas. Being at a college or university should not be one of them.

THE BERKELEY FREE SPEECH MOVEMENT

If universities and colleges were merely places where professional academics and students were committed to entering into the world of professional inquiry and discovery, it would be easy to establish norms of expression that protected ideas but also insisted on the respectful and professional exchange of positions. But campuses are not only that. Overlaid on top of this idea is a more general view that campuses should be open spaces, including for the noncivilized and nonscholarly expression of ideas. The event that established this norm was the Berkeley Free Speech Movement of the 1960s.

The Free Speech Movement (FSM) was a series of protests that occurred on the campus of the University of California, Berkeley, in 1964 and 1965.[70] Historically, the Berkeley campus had a policy of preventing student groups from using campus grounds for non-university-focused political activity or protest. Students would get around this prohibition by setting up tables and passing out leaflets on the city-owned sidewalk just on the edge of the campus. In the early 1960s a change in the campus border turned the sidewalk into university property, and the administration approved limited political activity on a small university-owned plaza at Bancroft Way and Telegraph Avenue. However, there was no strong consensus around this accommodation, and after reports that students were using this space to promote external protests (including one at the 1964 Republican National Convention in San Francisco), the dean of students told student groups they could no longer use the space to solicit support for "off campus political and social action."

Student groups responded with months of protests. Using the name Free Speech Movement, they attempted to get the administration to agree that the only limits on student activity and advocacy should be the limits of the Constitution, as interpreted by the courts. Rather than view the university as a heavily regulated space of professional instruction and scholarly activity, the students demanded that it also be recognized as a public forum for free speech. After a December 2 rally featuring the folk singer Joan Baez, many students occupied the administration building, leading to the arrest of

773 people. Many faculty members went to detention centers to retrieve students and bail them out. The following day the Academic Senate voted for no restrictions on the content of speech or advocacy.

These events precipitated what has become known as the "six-year war" on the Berkeley campus over free speech rights. The war involved students, faculty, administrators, Regents, legislators, and the former actor Ronald Reagan, who launched his political career in 1966 by targeting student activists and university leaders. During his successful run for governor Reagan vowed to send "the welfare bums back to work" and "clean up the mess at Berkeley." University of California president Clark Kerr, who resisted pressures to expel student activists, was fired three weeks after Reagan took office.[71] But even with this political backlash, the Berkeley Free Speech Movement helped establish within American higher education the rights of students to express themselves outside the academic context. As a result of the movement, student groups could use campus spaces to organize and advocate for political causes—a very different environment than existed in the 1950s. These precedents were especially consequential as students and others across the country asserted their right to protest the Vietnam War.

The AAUP approach to academic freedom was inextricably linked to professional standards and decorum; the FSM idea was not. The FSM insisted, and we agree, that campuses—public and private—must protect the freedom of the members of the academic community to use campus grounds for the broad expression of ideas, even if those ideas are expressed in ways that run contrary to the norms of professional conduct that apply within classrooms, scholarly gatherings, and department meetings.

We should think of campuses as having two different zones of free expression: a *professional zone*, which protects the expression of ideas but imposes an obligation of responsible discourse and responsible conduct in formal educational and scholarly settings; and a larger *free speech zone*, which exists outside scholarly and administrative settings and where the only restrictions are those of society at large. Members of the campus community may say things in the free speech zones that they would not be allowed to say in the core educational and research environment.[72]

We believe colleges and universities can almost never punish faculty members or students who express controversial views outside the professional, educational context, where there are no enforceable scholarly standards and no disruption of the educational context other than that certain persons may take offense. Faculty members who make controversial or even offensive statements on their Twitter feeds, but otherwise meet professional standards as teachers and colleagues, should not fear retaliation or harmful effects because of views they express outside their official duties. Similarly, students who are caught making controversial or even deeply offensive statements on their own time, but behave responsibly in the classroom and engage in no illegal harassment of others, cannot be officially penalized because of their offensive statements. Of course, like anyone who expresses controversial views, they will not be immune from criticism by others who also exercise their free speech rights. This means that Steven Salaita should not have been fired from the University of

Illinois because of some incendiary tweets during the 2014 Israel-Gaza crisis; by all accounts, his teaching and scholarship were unimpeachable.[73] A professor should not face sanctions for wearing blackface at an off-campus Halloween party.[74] A UCLA student who posted an internet video of a tirade against the Asian population at UCLA should not have to fear official reprisal as long as her behavior in the classroom and related settings was nondisruptive.[75]

Many will not easily agree to this; they want to see campuses do more to deal with offensive speech. There is a temptation to excommunicate faculty or students who, on their own time, express views that others in the campus community disapprove of. We saw this temptation even with our students, who were uncomfortable knowing that some people on campus might have said hateful things in other settings. But the Berkeley Free Speech Movement forced us all to draw a distinction between one's personal advocacy and one's participation in the scholarly and teaching mission of the university.

LESSONS LEARNED

The original 1915 AAUP document was later updated. The 1940 Statement of Principles on Academic Freedom and Tenure noted that "Institutions of higher education are conducted for the common good" and the "common good depends upon the free search for truth and its free exposition."[76] The updated summary of the basic tenets of academic freedom declared:

1. Teachers are entitled to full freedom in research and in the publication of the results, subject to

the adequate performance of their other academic duties. . . .

2. Teachers are entitled to freedom in the classroom in discussing their subject, but they should be careful not to introduce into their teaching controversial matter which has no relation to their subject. . . .

3. College and university teachers are citizens, members of a learned profession, and officers of an educational institution. When they speak or write as citizens, they should be free from institutional censorship or discipline, but their special position in the community imposes special obligations . . . [to] at all times be accurate, exercise appropriate restraint, show respect for the opinions of others, and make every effort to indicate that they are not speaking for the institution.[77]

When the statement was updated again in 1970 in the wake of the Free Speech Movement, it included a new footnote saying that "teachers are citizens and should be accorded the freedom of citizens" and "a faculty member's expression of opinion as a citizen cannot constitute grounds for dismissal unless it clearly demonstrates the faculty member's unfitness for his or her position."[78]

Our view goes ever further than this. The AAUP still contemplates that a faculty member's private expression may itself (rarely but possibly) demonstrate the faculty member's unfitness for his or her position. But the history we have just reviewed shows that there have been too many times when the political views of faculty—such as those who supported unions in the 1890s, opposed World War I in the 1910s, or sympathized with the teachings of Marx in the 1930s, 1940s, and 1950s—were treated as proof of unfitness. Colleges and universities can resist the temptation to evaluate ideological fitness by focusing on the straightforward question of whether faculty members are meeting their professional obligations as teachers, scholars, and colleagues. Statements by a faculty member may give rise to an inquiry, but a finding of unfitness cannot be based solely on a person's controversial or offensive statements or views.

This is not only our view. In 1967, the United States Supreme Court addressed academic freedom in *Keyishian v. Board of Regents*. Harry Keyishian was an instructor in English at the State University of New York at Buffalo who objected to being forced by his administration, as a condition of his continued employment, to deny that he had ever been a member of the Communist Party. He believed his private political views should have no bearing on whether he was qualified to be a professor at the university. The Supreme Court agreed, stating forcefully that "academic freedom . . . is of transcendent value to all of us and not merely to the teachers concerned. That freedom is therefore a special concern of the First Amendment, which does not tolerate laws that cast a pall of orthodoxy over the classroom."[79]

The history of free speech is the history of a long, difficult, and fragile movement to establish greater protections in society for ideas considered harmful or offensive. That struggle has yielded extraordinary benefits. The history of academic freedom shows that these values have an even more vital role to play in those institutions that are dedicated to nurturing new ideas, challenging prevailing orthodoxies, and providing society with the best possible example of how to encourage independent thinking and engage in rigorous assessment. Ronald Dworkin expressed this well:

> Liberal public education, freedom of speech, conscience, and religion, and academic freedom are all parts of our society's support for a culture of independence and of its defense against a culture of conformity. Academic freedom plays a special role because educational institutions are pivotal to those efforts. They are pivotal, first, because they can so easily become engines of conformity, as every totalitarian regime has realized, and, second, because they can provide important encouragement and skills for a life of personal conviction. Part of the point of education, in a liberal society, is learning the importance and depth of an allegiance to personal rather than collective truth. . . . In no other occupation is it so plainly and evidently the responsibility of professionals to find and tell and teach the truth as they see it. Scholars exist for that, and only for that.[80]

This is the foundational idea. Still, even if we acknowledge that disciplined free thinkers (scholars and students) deserve special consideration, it is possible to argue that certain kinds of speech acts, which attack and demean people for ugly, hateful reasons, should nevertheless have no place in higher education.

CHAPTER FOUR

Hate Speech

I<small>F</small> all ideas, no matter how offensive, should be expressible on college campuses, what about epithets based on race, sex, religion or sexual orientation? What about the expression of hate more generally? Many prominent scholars have argued that hate speech conveys nothing useful to the marketplace of ideas, and by silencing its victims, it limits the exchange of ideas and undermines a university's obligation to provide all students with an environment conducive to learning.[1]

In the 1990s, persuaded by the powerful arguments for its regulation, over 350 colleges and universities adopted codes restricting hate speech. But every court to consider such a code declared it unconstitutional.[2] In this matter we side with the courts: though the advocates of restricting hate speech were motivated by the best intentions, speech cannot and should not be prohibited for expressing hate. We strongly agree with the need to create a conducive learning environment for all students, but there is simply no way to regulate hate speech without censoring ideas. That is never permissible on college campuses.

THE HARMS OF HATE SPEECH

If speech never mattered, there would be no reason to safeguard it. Freedom of speech is protected as a fundamental right precisely because speech may have powerful effects. Sometimes these effects are enormously positive; a democracy could not function without the ability to criticize government policy and openly discuss political candidates. But it is naïve and wrong to pretend that speech cannot also cause great harm. Many scholars have persuasively argued that the harm inflicted by hate speech is great enough to justify regulating it.

At the outset, a definitional question: what is hate speech? Jeremy Waldron defines it as "the use of words which are deliberately abusive and/or insulting and/or threatening and/or demeaning directed at members of vulnerable minorities, calculated to stir up hatred against them."[3] He notes with approval that laws controlling such speech

> can be found in Canada, Denmark, Germany, New Zealand, and the United Kingdom, prohibiting public statements that "incite hatred against any identifiable group where such incitements are likely to lead to a breach of the peace" (Canada); or statements "by which a group of people are degraded because of their race, colour of skin, national or ethnic background" (Denmark); or attacks on "the human dignity of others by insulting, maliciously

maligning or defaming segments of the population"
(Germany); or "threatening, abusive, or insulting . . . words
likely to excite hostility against or bring into contempt any
group of persons on the ground of colour, race, or ethnic
origins . . ."; or the use of "threatening, abusive, or insulting words or behavior when these are intended to stir up
racial hatred" (United Kingdom).[4]

Waldron and others offer several reasons why such hate
speech should be regulated, especially in colleges and universities. First, it causes psychological and even physical harm to
those who are subjected to it. Richard Delgado writes: "In
addition to the harms of immediate emotional distress and
infringement of dignity, racial insults inflict psychological
harm upon the victim. Racial slurs may cause long-term emotional pain because they draw upon and intensify the effects
of the stigmatization, labeling, and disrespectful treatment
that the victim has previously undergone."[5] Mari Matsuda
adds: "Victims of vicious hate propaganda experience psychological symptoms and emotional distress ranging from fear
in the gut to rapid pulse rate and difficulty in breathing,
nightmares, post-traumatic stress syndrome, stress disorder,
hypertension, psychosis, and suicide. Patricia Williams has
called the blows of racist messages 'spirit murder' in recognition of the psychic destruction victims experience."[6]

Second, hate speech is an affront to the dignity of those
who are subjected to it. Waldron argues that regulating hate
speech is not about stopping offense, but rather protecting
the dignity of each individual. He believes that in a "well-
ordered society," all people not only must be protected by the
law, but are entitled to live in confidence of this protection.

"Each person . . . should be able to go about his or her business, with the assurance that there will be no need to face hostility, violence, discrimination or exclusion by others."[7] Hate speech undermines confidence in the law's protection. "When a society is defaced with anti-Semitic signage, burning crosses and defamatory racial leaflets," Waldron says, the assurance of security "evaporates."[8] "A vigilant police force and a Justice Department may still keep people from being attacked or excluded," but the objects of hate speech are deprived of the assurance that the society regards them as people of equal dignity.[9] He says that the "aim" of hate speech "is to compromise the dignity of those at whom it is targeted, both in their own eyes and in the eyes of members of society."[10] Delgado likewise writes that "a racial insult is always a dignitary affront, a direct violation of the victim's right to be treated respectfully."[11]

Third, hate speech is a form of discrimination and should not be allowed any more than any other discrimination. Hate speech subordinates minorities. At colleges and universities, it causes its victims to feel unwelcome and interferes with their education. Charles Lawrence, in a widely cited article, explains: "Racism is both 100 percent speech and 100 percent conduct. . . . All racist speech constructs the social reality that constrains the liberty of nonwhites because of their race. By limiting the life opportunities of others, this act of constructing meaning also makes racist speech conduct."[12] Catharine MacKinnon, who urged the prohibition of pornography because it subordinates women, said: "The law of equality and the law of freedom of speech are on a collision course in this country. . . . The constitutional doctrine of free speech has developed without taking equality seriously."[13]

Fourth, it is argued that hate speech is an assault that the law can and should prevent and punish. Lawrence writes: "The experience of being called 'nigger,' 'spic,' 'Jap,' or 'kike' is like receiving a slap in the face. The injury is instantaneous. There is neither an opportunity for intermediary reflection on the idea conveyed nor an opportunity for responsive speech."[14] Like a physical assault, hate speech silences its victims. Lawrence goes on: "Words like 'nigger,' 'kike,' and 'faggot' produce physical symptoms that temporarily disable the victim, and perpetrators often use these words with the intention of producing this effect. . . . The subordinated victims of fighting words also are silenced by their relatively powerless position in society."[15]

Most democratic nations prohibit hate speech. As one commentator noted, "the United States stands virtually alone in thinking that hate speech ought to be protected."[16] The Race Relations Act in the United Kingdom, for example, makes it a crime to publish or distribute "threatening, abusive, or insulting" written material or to use such language in a public place.[17] In Germany, *Volksverhetzung*—"incitement of popular hatred"—is an offense under Section 130 of the Strafgesetzbuch (Germany's criminal code) punishable by up to five years' imprisonment. Section 130 makes it a crime to publicly incite hatred against parts of the population, to call for violent or arbitrary measures against them, or to insult, maliciously slur, or defame them in a manner violating their human dignity.

As we listened to our students describe their experiences with hate speech, we understood why they wanted to restrict it. The effects described by Delgado, Lawrence, Matsuda,

Waldron, and others are real. Hate speech genuinely threatens an inclusive learning environment, and colleges and universities are right in wishing to protect this environment.

THE FIRST AMENDMENT AND THE EXPRESSION OF HATE

Throughout American history, powerful arguments have been advanced for restricting speech that is considered harmful, and we have learned the advantages of extending free speech protections even in the face of legitimate concerns about harm. How do general free speech principles and the current state of First Amendment law apply to hate speech?

Although the Supreme Court has never ruled on whether colleges or universities may prohibit the expression of hate, the Court's decisions have touched on issues of hateful expression in four areas: group libel, fighting words, laws prohibiting cross burning, and statutes imposing greater penalties for hate-motivated crimes. Taken together, these decisions make it very difficult for public colleges or universities to constitutionally prohibit hateful expression. Of course, that does not address whether this *should* be the law and whether private colleges and universities, which are not bound by the First Amendment, should follow the same approach. Before we get to that question, however, consider what the Supreme Court has said about hateful expression.

Group Libel

More than a half century ago, the Supreme Court held that group libel is not protected by the First Amendment. In

Beauharnais v. Illinois (1952), the Court upheld a state law that prohibited any publication portraying "depravity, criminality, unchastity, or lack of virtue of a class of citizens, of any race, color, creed, or religion [which exposes such citizens] to contempt, derision, or obloquy or which is productive of breach of the peace or riots."[18] Justice Felix Frankfurter's opinion affirmed the conviction of individuals who had urged the Mayor and City Council of Chicago to protect white neighborhoods from "encroachment, harassment, and invasion . . . by the Negro" and who called for "one million self respecting white people in Chicago to unite."[19]

Just as a state can punish defamation against an individual, wrote Frankfurter, so may it "punish the same utterance directed at a defined group."[20] Noting the strife caused by expressions of hate based on race and religion, he concluded that the government did not need to show that these expressions posed a "clear and present danger" because "libelous utterances not being within the area of constitutionally protected speech, it is unnecessary, either for us or for the State courts, to consider the issues behind the phrase 'clear and present danger.' "[21]

Beauharnais is the strongest authority for the government to regulate racist speech, and it has never been overruled. Yet it is very questionable whether it is still good law.[22] It was decided at a time when the Court considered any type of defamatory speech to be outside the protection of the First Amendment—a premise the Court expressly rejected a decade later in *New York Times v. Sullivan*, when the justices ruled in favor of civil rights advocates who were being sued for defamation by Southern segregationists.[23] The speech at issue in *Beauharnais*, however vile, was political speech, and it is highly doubtful that the Court today would allow punishment of individuals for expressing opinions about racial groups or calling for government actions.[24] In fact, a later decision, *R.A.V. v. City of St. Paul*, in 1992, strongly indicates that expression of hate is not entirely outside First Amendment protection.[25] As discussed below, there the Court declared unconstitutional a law prohibiting burning a cross or painting a swastika in a manner likely to cause "anger, alarm, or resentment." Moreover, the Illinois statute upheld in *Beauharnais* almost certainly would be declared unconstitutional today on grounds of vagueness and overbreadth.

A reflection of the abandonment of *Beauharnais* is found in the protection of Nazis' right to stage a march in the predominantly Jewish suburb of Skokie, Illinois. In 1977, the leaders of the Nationalist Socialist Party of America announced that they planned to hold a peaceful demonstration in Skokie, a town with many survivors of Nazi concentration camps. A trial court issued an injunction preventing the marchers from wearing Nazi uniforms, displaying swastikas, or expressing hatred toward Jewish people. The court relied in part on testimony concerning a large counter-demonstration and the fear of a violent confrontation between the two groups. Although the state appellate courts upheld this injunction, the United States Supreme Court summarily reversed the state courts.[26] The Illinois Court of Appeals then modified the injunction so that it prohibited only display of the swastika. The Illinois Supreme Court vacated the entire injunction as violating the First Amendment.[27]

Meanwhile, Skokie adopted several ordinances meant to prevent the Nazis from speaking there. These laws required applicants for parade permits to purchase a substantial amount of insurance, prohibited dissemination of material that "promotes and incites hatred" based on race or religion, and outlawed wearing military-style uniforms in demonstrations. The United States Court of Appeals for the Seventh Circuit declared these ordinances unconstitutional and expressly said that it no longer regarded *Beauharnais* as good law.[28] After winning in the courts, the Nazi party canceled its rally in Skokie and held a small protest march in Chicago.

The Skokie controversy reflects many basic First Amendment principles. The courts ruled that expression of hate is protected speech, and the government may not outlaw symbols of hate such as swastikas. Moreover, the government cannot suppress a speaker because of an anticipated audience reaction. Skokie was not allowed to prevent the Nazis from marching even though their demonstration would deeply offend and upset Holocaust survivors and might even provoke a violent response. The Skokie litigation and other developments in First Amendment law since *Beauharnais* make it very difficult to argue that campuses can prohibit hate speech as a form of group libel.

Fighting Words

Another approach that government might take to banning hate speech is by considering it a form of fighting words. Many colleges and universities have based their hate speech codes around the fighting words exception to the First Amendment. Professor Lawrence used this argument to claim that colleges and universities can prohibit hate speech.[29]

In the 1942 case *Chaplinsky v. New Hampshire*, the Supreme Court expressly held that "fighting words" are unprotected by the First Amendment.[30] Chaplinsky, a Jehovah's Witness, was distributing literature for his religion on a street corner on a Saturday afternoon and gave a speech denouncing other religions as a "racket." He said at one point to a listener, "You are a God damned racketeer" and "a damned Fascist and the whole government of Rochester are Fascists or agents of Fascists."[31]

The Supreme Court upheld Chaplinsky's conviction for this speech, saying that "allowing the broadest scope to the language and purpose of the Fourteenth Amendment, it is well understood that the right of free speech is not absolute at all times and under all circumstances. There are certain well-defined and narrowly limited classes of speech, the prevention and punishment of which have never been thought to raise any constitutional problem. These include the lewd and obscene, the profane, the libelous, and *the insulting or fighting words—those which by their very utterance inflict injury or tend to incite an immediate breach of the peace.*"[32] The Court said that "such utterances are no essential part of any exposition of ideas, and are of such slight social value as a step to truth that any benefit that may be derived from them is clearly outweighed by the social interest in order and morality. Resort to epithets or personal abuse is not in any proper sense communication of information or opinion safeguarded by the Constitution."[33]

Chaplinsky appears to recognize two situations where speech constitutes fighting words: when the speech is likely to cause a violent response against the speaker, and when it is an insult likely to inflict immediate emotional harm. Each aspect raises questions. As to the danger that the listener will be provoked to fight, the issue is whether the appropriate response is to punish the speaker or punish the person who actually resorts to violence. A physical reaction against a speaker should not be a basis for silencing the speaker; otherwise, it is too easy for people to silence the speech they don't like by threatening a reaction against it.

As to the infliction of emotional injury, the question—which is key in the discussion of hate speech—is whether any speech should be punished because it is upsetting or deeply offensive to an audience.[34] Expression of ideas—for example, that a racial or ethnic group is inferior—also can inflict immediate emotional harm. Depending on the audience, speech expressing all types of ideas can inflict emotional distress. In the early 1960s, there is no doubt that civil rights protests deeply upset those who believed in segregation. Donald Trump's promise if elected to deport those not lawfully in the United States upset those who have to live in fear of deportation. Allowing speech to be censored or punished because it causes an immediate emotional reaction gives the government an unlimited power to restrict expression.

The Supreme Court has never overturned *Chaplinsky;* fighting words remain unprotected by the First Amendment. But in the more than seventy years since that decision, the Court has never again upheld a fighting words conviction. It has used three techniques in overturning these convictions.

First, in *Cohen v. California* (1971), the Court narrowed the scope of the fighting words doctrine by ruling that it applies only to speech directed at another person that is likely to produce a violent response.[35] Cohen was convicted of disturbing the peace for wearing in a courthouse a jacket with the words "Fuck the Draft." The state argued, in part, that the inscription on the jacket constituted fighting words because it might provoke violence from people who were angered by the message. In an opinion by Justice John Harlan, the Court rejected this reasoning: "While the four-letter word displayed by Cohen in relation to the draft is not uncommonly employed in a personally provocative fashion, in this instance it was clearly not directed to the person of the hearer. No individual actually or likely to be present could reasonably have regarded the words on appellant's jacket as a direct personal insult."[36]

The Court also applied this requirement in *Texas v. Johnson* (1989), where it held that flag burning, though deeply offensive to many, was a form of speech protected by the First Amendment.[37] One argument made by the government was that flag burning was likely to provoke a violent response from those who saw it and thus was a form of fighting words. Justice William Brennan's majority opinion rejected this contention for the reason given in *Cohen:* "No reasonable onlooker would have regarded [the] generalized expression of dissatisfaction with the policies of the Federal Government as a direct personal insult or an invitation to exchange fisticuffs."[38]

Second, the Court has often found laws prohibiting fighting words to be unconstitutionally vague or overbroad. *Gooding v. Wilson* (1972) involved an individual who was convicted for saying to a police officer at an antiwar demonstration, "White son of a bitch, I'll kill you," and "You son of a bitch, I'll choke you to death."[39] He was convicted under a Georgia law that forbade any person to "use to or of another, and in his presence opprobrious words or abusive language, tending to cause a breach of the peace."[40] The Court found that the statute's definition of fighting words would impermissibly allow for the prosecution of clearly protected speech. Three other cases decided that same year—*Rosenfeld v. New Jersey*,[41] *Lewis v. City of New Orleans*,[42] and *Brown v. Oklahoma*[43]—also involved the angry use of profanity in a manner likely to provoke an audience. In each case, the Court overturned the conviction.

Third, the Court has declared it impermissible to pass laws prohibiting some fighting words but not others. This was the result in *R.A.V. v. City of St. Paul* (1992), one of the Court's most important cases about hate speech.[44] A St. Paul ordinance prohibited placing "on public or private property symbols, objects, characterizations, or graffiti, including, but not limited to, a burning cross or Nazi swastika, which one knows or has reasonable grounds to know arouses anger, alarm or resentment in others on the basis of race, color, creed, religion or gender."[45] The Minnesota Supreme Court gave the ordinance a narrow construction so that it applied only to fighting words or incitement not protected by the First Amendment.

All nine Justices on the United States Supreme Court voted to declare the ordinance unconstitutional and overturn the conviction of a man who burned a cross on a black family's lawn. Justice Scalia noted that "the exclusion of fighting words from First Amendment protection means that they are regarded as essentially a 'nonspeech' element of communication," like "a noisy sound truck." But as with a sound truck, he added, "The government may not regulate use based on hostility—or favoritism—towards the underlying message expressed."[46] The problem with the St. Paul ordinance was that it drew content-based distinctions among expressions of hate: it prohibited hate speech based on race, religion, or gender, but not based on political affiliation or sexual orientation. Justice Scalia pointed out: "Displays containing abusive invective, no matter how vicious or severe, are permissible unless they are addressed to one of the specified disfavored topics. Those who wish to use 'fighting words' in connection with other ideas—to express hostility, for example, on the basis of political affiliation, union membership, or homosexuality—are not covered."[47]

The Court has created a Catch-22 when it comes to the regulation of so-called fighting words: a law punishing fighting words in general will be struck down as too broad and vague (that is, it covers too much), but a narrower law, focusing just on certain kinds of fighting words, will be struck down as an illegitimate content-based distinction (that is, it covers too little). While the fighting words exception technically still exists within First Amendment law,[48] this Catch-22, combined with the fact that the justices have never upheld a fighting words conviction in all the years since *Chaplinsky*, makes it virtually impossible for public colleges and universities to regulate hate speech on these grounds.

Cross Burning

In *Virginia v. Black* (2003), the Court held that governments may prohibit cross burning when it is intended to intimidate, but this intent must be proven in the particular case; in other words, the mere act of burning a cross is not inherently unprotected speech.[49] A Virginia law prohibited cross burning "with an intent to intimidate a person or group of persons." The law also described an act of cross burning as "prima facie evidence of an intent to intimidate a person or group of persons." In evaluating the law, the Court simultaneously considered two separate cases: one involving Klan members who were convicted of burning a cross at a rally on an isolated farm, and the other involving two men who were convicted of burning a cross on the lawn of a home recently purchased by an African American family.

The Court's holding had three parts. First, the government cannot prohibit all cross burning. Justice Sandra Day O'Connor, writing for the majority in an 8–1 decision, explained that burning a cross is symbolic expression, and the government cannot ban symbols just because they are powerful and offensive. Second, cross burning as a means of communicating a serious intent to commit an act of unlawful violence to a particular individual or group of individuals— what is known in the law as a "true threat"—is not protected by the First Amendment.[50] Third, there must be proof in the individual case that the speech was a true threat. The Court concluded that the Klan members could not be punished for burning a cross on an isolated farm because the absence of onlookers meant that the action could not reasonably be seen as a true threat. But the Court made clear that the men who had burned a cross on an African American family's lawn could be convicted because this act obviously was a true threat.

By concluding that cross burning generally is protected speech, the Court prevents public colleges and universities from treating expression of hate as inherently punishable. But by allowing punishment of such speech in the context of a true threat, the Court does provide opportunities for campuses to deal with certain kinds of hateful acts.

Penalty Enhancements for Hate-Motivated Crimes

The final area where the Court has considered hate speech is in the context of laws that provide enhanced penalties for hate-motivated crimes. In *Wisconsin v. Mitchell* (1993), the Court upheld a state law that imposed greater punishments if it could be proved that a victim was chosen because of his or her race.[51] The Supreme Court emphasized that these penalty enhancements are directed at conduct, not at speech, and that they are justified because "bias-motivated crimes are more likely to provoke retaliatory crimes, inflict distinct emotional harms on their victims, and incite community unrest. The State's desire to redress these perceived harms provides an adequate explanation for its penalty-enhancement provision over and above mere disagreement with offenders' beliefs or biases."[52] This logic is similar to that in employment discrimination cases, where the prohibition is focused on bad conduct but speech acts may be part of the proof that bad conduct took place. In that sense, these cases do not provide a legal basis for regulating hate speech.

THE EXPERIENCE WITH HATE SPEECH CODES

This history allows us to understand the legal fate of previous efforts to pass hate speech codes. By the early 1990s, over 350 colleges and universities adopted hate speech codes. A number of these were challenged in court, and all to be challenged were declared unconstitutional.[53]

One of the most prominent examples involved the University of Michigan, which was motivated to devise a hate speech code after some truly horrendous events on campus.[54] In 1987, flyers were distributed that declared "open season" on blacks. Blacks were referred to as "saucer lips," "porch monkeys," and "jigaboos." A student disc jockey allowed racist jokes to be broadcast on the campus radio station, and student demonstrations were interrupted by the display of a KKK uniform from a nearby dorm window. Another flyer proclaimed, "Niggers get off campus" and "Darkies don't belong in classrooms—they belong hanging from trees." The university had to respond to such horrific expression.

The challenge was how to translate the natural desire to eliminate such egregious behavior into a policy that was consistent with the First Amendment. This proved extremely difficult. The policy adopted by the university in 1988 prohibited:

> Any behavior, verbal or physical, that stigmatizes or victimizes an individual on the basis of race, ethnicity, religion, sex, sexual orientation, creed, national origin, ancestry, age, marital status, handicap or Vietnam-era veteran status, and that
>
> a. Involves an express or implied threat to an individual's academic efforts, employment, participation in University sponsored extra-curricular activities or personal safety; or
> b. Has the purpose or reasonably foreseeable effect of interfering with an individual's academic efforts, employment, participation in University sponsored extra-curricular activities or personal safety; or
> c. Creates an intimidating, hostile, or demeaning environment for educational pursuits, employment or participation in University sponsored extra-curricular activities.[55]

Shortly after this policy went into effect, in the fall of 1988, the University Office of Affirmative Action issued an interpretive guide entitled *What Students Should Know about Discrimination and Discriminatory Harassment by Students in the University Environment.* The examples of what was prohibited included:

> A flyer containing racist threats distributed in a residence hall.
>
> Racist graffiti written on the door of an Asian student's study carrel.
>
> A male student makes remarks in class like "Women just aren't as good in this field as men," thus creating a hostile learning atmosphere for female classmates.
>
> Students in a residence hall have a floor party and invite everyone on their floor except one person because they think she might be a lesbian.
>
> A black student is confronted and racially insulted by two white students in a cafeteria.
>
> Male students leave pornographic pictures and jokes on the desk of a female graduate student.
>
> Two men demand that their roommate in the residence hall move out and be tested for AIDS.[56]

Commenting on the breadth of this code, Kent Greenawalt observed that it "seemed to reach into the realm of obnoxious ideas civilly expressed."[57]

In practice, the code was used not against the kinds of purely hateful slurs that inspired its passage, but against people who expressed opinions that others objected to.

Complaints were filed against a student who stated that Jewish people used the Holocaust to justify Israel's policies toward the Palestinians. Another student found himself facing punishment for saying that he had heard that minorities had a difficult time in a particular course. A graduate student in social work was subjected to formal disciplinary procedures for asserting that homosexuality was a disease.[58] As the court noted, "On at least three separate occasions, students were disciplined or threatened with discipline for comments made in a classroom setting."[59] Eventually, a graduate student challenged the policy in federal court by claiming that the hate speech code put him at risk of punishment for studying certain controversial theories in his field of psychobiology, including the study of individual and group differences in personality traits and cognitive abilities.

A federal judge struck down the policy on the grounds that the University of Michigan's definition of what was prohibited speech was so broad and vague that it was "simply impossible to discern any limitation" on the policy's reach.[60] Any controversial or critical comment could put someone at risk for punishment. To qualify as prohibited under the code, the judge wrote, language must " 'stigmatize' or 'victimize' an individual. However, both of these terms are general and elude precise definition. Moreover, it is clear that the fact that a statement may victimize or stigmatize an individual does not, in and of itself, strip it of protection under the accepted First Amendment tests."[61]

This was not an isolated outcome. Between 1989 and 1995, every court that examined a university speech code found the code unconstitutional. The hate speech code passed by the University of Wisconsin, for instance,[62] provided that the university could discipline a student in nonacademic matters in the following situations:

> For racist or discriminatory comments, epithets or other expressive behavior directed at an individual or on separate occasions at different individuals, or for physical conduct, if such comments, epithets or other expressive behavior or physical conduct intentionally:
> 1. Demean the race, sex, religion, color, creed, disability, sexual orientation, national origin, ancestry or age of the individual or individuals; and
> 2. Create an intimidating, hostile or demeaning environment for education, university-related work, or other university-authorized activity.[63]

The federal district court found this regulation unconstitutionally overbroad and vague, mostly because a great deal of speech that people might consider "demeaning" was clearly protected by the First Amendment.

When George Mason University suspended a fraternity in 1991 after it conducted an "ugly woman contest" with racist and sexist overtones, the United States Court of Appeals struck down the sanctions, explaining that the First Amendment protected even offensive and juvenile expression. The court declared: "We agree wholeheartedly that it is the University officials' responsibility, even their obligation, to achieve the goals they have set. On the other hand, a public university has many constitutionally permissible means to protect female and minority students. We must emphasize, as have other courts, that 'the manner of [its action] cannot consist of selective limitations upon speech.' "[64]

The invalidation of hate speech codes was not limited to public universities. In May 1990, the Stanford Student Conduct Legislative Council adopted a student conduct code, drafted by law professor and constitutional scholar Thomas Grey, that prohibited "discriminatory harassment," including "personal vilification of students on the basis of their sex, race, color, handicap, religion, sexual orientation or national and ethnic origin."[65] Personal vilification was defined as intentional, personally directed "fighting words or non-verbal symbols . . . commonly understood to convey direct and visceral hatred or contempt for human beings" on the basis of their membership in those groups.[66]

In February 1995, a California Superior Court judge invalidated the Stanford code as violating a California statute, the Leonard Law, which provides that "no private postsecondary educational institution shall make or enforce any rule subjecting any student to disciplinary sanctions solely on the basis of conduct that is speech . . . that, when engaged in outside the campus or facility of a private postsecondary institution, is protected from governmental restriction by the First Amendment."[67] The Leonard Law thus says that private schools cannot punish speech that would be deemed protected in a public institution. The court declared: "Defendants' Speech Code does violate Plaintiffs' 1st Amendment rights since the Speech Code proscribes more than just 'fighting words' as defined in *Chaplinsky*, and the later lines of case law. To this extent, therefore, Defendants' Speech Code is overbroad. In addition, however, the Speech Code also targets the content of certain speech [and] . . . is an impermissible content-based regulation."[68]

The motivations behind the desire to punish hateful speech are laudable. So far, however, the legal and definitional challenges of translating these motivations into workable codes have proven impossible to overcome. After watching so many universities lose in court, some, such as the University of Pennsylvania, withdrew their hate speech codes; others, such as Yale, said they would not be enforced.[69]

SHOULD HATE SPEECH ON CAMPUSES BE PROHIBITED?

We believe, with legal scholars Delgado, Lawrence, Matsuda, and Waldron, that hate speech causes great harm and that colleges and universities must act to protect students from harm. Their advocacy was instrumental in causing many schools to adopt policies prohibiting such expression. But the courts have ruled that the First Amendment clearly prohibits public colleges and universities from using hate speech codes to achieve this goal.

This is the law. But should it be? After all, many countries punish speech that disparages or incites hatred against a person or group on the basis of race, religion, sex, ethnicity, or sexual orientation. Even if public colleges and universities are limited by First Amendment restrictions, there might still be good reasons why private colleges and universities should adopt such codes.

We think not. There are strong reasons why campuses should resist calls to censor and punish people who express ideas considered offensive, hateful, or demeaning.

First, decades and decades of efforts—by state governments, local municipalities, and campuses—have demonstrated that all such codes are impermissibly vague and overbroad. They all risk punishing people based on political viewpoint or worldview. Any rule that seeks to punish people for their speech must state specifically what is prohibited and what is allowed. Otherwise, too many people will be afraid to say anything controversial for fear that they will be singled out for arbitrary punishment based on unclear standards. There are no examples of codes that both are sufficiently specific and that apply only to unprotected speech. The Michigan code, for instance, prohibited "any behavior, verbal or physical, that stigmatizes or victimizes an individual on the basis of race, ethnicity, religion, sex, sexual orientation, creed." The Stanford code provided that "Speech or other expression constitutes harassment by vilification if it: a) is intended to insult or stigmatize an individual or individuals on the basis of their sex, race, color, handicap, religion, sexual orientation, or national and ethnic origin."[70] The University of Wisconsin code prohibited speech that was "demeaning" based on "race, sex, religion, color, creed, disability, sexual orientation, national origin, ancestry or age of the individual or individuals." Jeremy Waldron defined hate speech as "the use of words which are deliberately abusive and/ or insulting and/or threatening and/or demeaning directed at members of vulnerable minorities, calculated to stir up hatred against them."[71]

These codes have an intentionally broad sweep, but precisely for that reason, they inevitably prohibit the expression of ideas that might be seen as "stigmatizing," "demeaning," or "insulting." In addition to being inherently vague, these concepts are also inherently politically charged. Much of what we debate as a society—including on college campuses—relates to whether certain forms of expression should be considered demeaning or insulting, and these disagreements often run deep. Many anti-racism and anti-sexism advocates make powerful arguments for why seemingly innocuous speech acts, and many forms of cultural expression, should be considered exclusionary and demeaning. Some even embrace the view that cultural reproduction of racism and patriarchy is built into the very foundation of our social order. Opponents of these positions sometimes claim the critics are too quick to find oppression, that they are humorless, or that their concerns, while sometimes legitimate, are overstated. Others argue that what the critics consider demeaning (such as sexualized depictions of women or certain examples of cultural appropriation) are actually empowering. The arguments are endless.

Given this level of disagreement, any hate speech code can, in theory, either lead to the punishment of very many people (who may not think they are demeaning anyone) or result in a refusal to punish many arguably stigmatizing speech acts. The upshot is that people will inevitably be punished for their political views, with arbitrary and often surprising results. Given the definitional problems, how could it be otherwise? Suppose gay and lesbian students complain that they are demeaned by a Christian student's expressed belief that traditional heterosexual marriage is the only true marriage. Should the university deny that this belief is demeaning, or punish the student? What if the Christian student then complains that the gay students' complaint demeans and stigmatizes her religious beliefs? The door is open to an endless succession of claims and counterclaims. Justice Clarence Thomas believes that affirmative action programs stigmatize minorities on the basis of race and "stamp minorities with a badge of inferiority."[72] Could a student's advocacy of affirmative action be taken as stigmatizing minorities as inferior? What of Laura Kipnis's argument that overly protective approaches to sex on campus stigmatize women? Or the claim that some anti-racism rhetoric demeans whites and is calculated to stir up hatred against them? These challenges are inherent to the entire enterprise. They cannot be solved with better definitions.

This brings us to our second argument against such codes: they are often used to punish the speech of people who were not their intended targets. Vague and overbroad laws inherently risk discriminatory enforcement, and that is exactly what has happened with hate speech codes. As Nadine Strossen observes: "One ironic, even tragic, result of this discretion is that members of minority groups themselves—the very people whom the law is intended to protect—are likely targets of punishment. For example, among the first individuals prosecuted under the British Race Relations Act of 1965 were black power leaders."[73] Although the English law was adopted in response to a rise in anti-Semitic incidents on campus, it was used against those who advocated on behalf of Israel, by people who argued that according to United Nations General Assembly resolution no. 3379, Zionism was a form of racism.[74]

That has also been the experience with hate speech codes in the United States. As Henry Louis Gates Jr. notes:

> During the years in which Michigan's speech code was enforced, more than twenty blacks were charged—by whites—with racist speech. Not a single instance of white

racist speech was punished. . . . A full disciplinary hearing was conducted only in the case of a black social work student who was charged with saying, in a class discussion of research projects, that he believed that homosexuality was an illness, and that he was developing a social work approach to move homosexuals toward heterosexuality.[75]

Hate speech codes around the world have often been applied in politically charged ways. In 2006, individuals in Sweden were convicted for distributing leaflets to high school students saying homosexuality was a "deviant sexual proclivity," had "a morally destructive effect on the substance of society," and was responsible for the development of HIV and AIDS.[76] In 2009, a member of the Belgian Parliament was convicted of distributing leaflets with the slogans "Stand up against the Islamification of Belgium," "Stop the sham integration policy," and "Send non-European job seekers home."[77] The European Court of Human Rights affirmed these convictions, rejecting defenses based on freedom of speech.[78] In Poland, a Catholic magazine was fined $11,000 for inciting "contempt, hostility and malice" by comparing a woman's abortion to the medical experiments at Auschwitz.[79] In 2008, film star Brigitte Bardot was convicted by French authorities for placing online a letter to president Nicolas Sarkozy in which she complained about the Islamic practice of ritual animal slaughter. It was her fifth conviction for hate speech.[80] In 2011, Scottish football fan Stephen Birrell was sentenced to eight months in prison for insulting Celtic F.C. fans, Catholics, and the pope on a Facebook page. During sentencing, the sheriff, Bill Totten, told Birrell that his views would not be tolerated by "the right-thinking people of Glasgow and Scotland."[81] In Kenya, hate speech laws are used only against those who speak out against the ruling party's Jubilee Alliance, including a movement leader who contested the 2013 election results, a student activist who criticized the president on Twitter, and a blogger who said the president was "adolescent."[82]

We come back to a central point: protecting hate speech is necessary because the alternative—granting governments the power to punish speakers they don't like—creates even more harm. The argument in favor of hate speech laws is essentially an argument for granting people in authority the power to censor or punish individuals who insult, stigmatize, or demean others, and it is inevitable that such vague and broad authority will be abused or used in ways that were not contemplated by censorship advocates.

Even if one could punish exactly the hateful speakers one hopes to punish, the entire process risks making martyrs and rallying support for those sanctioned. For example, the Dutch government's hate speech prosecutions of far-right politician Geertz Wilders led to more attention to his anti-Muslim sentiments and his criticisms of Moroccan immigrants. It allowed him to motivate the increasing ranks of his supporters by claiming that "If speaking about this is punishable, then the Netherlands is no longer a free country but a dictatorship." (One of his tweets reads, "Prosecuted for what millions think.")[83] Moreover, as Strossen notes, these bans can stultify "the candid intergroup dialogue concerning racism and other forms of bias that constitutes an essential precondition for reducing discrimination" and can "generate litigation and other forms of controversy that will exacerbate intergroup tensions."[84]

There is also no evidence that the presence or absence of hate speech laws results in more tolerant attitudes toward vulnerable groups or in less discrimination. In the United States, even without hate speech laws, we have moved from only 4 percent of Americans approving of interracial marriage in 1958 to 86 percent approval in 2011, with about 15 percent of all new marriages in 2015 between persons of different races. According to FBI statistics, the total number of U.S. hate crime incidents decreased from 8,759 in 1996 to 6,628 in 2010 and to 5,928 in 2015. Even without punishing anti-gay sentiment, acceptance of same-sex marriage has dramatically increased between 2001 (when 57 percent of people opposed it) to 2016 (when 55 percent favored it), mostly because of the greater presence of gay and lesbian voices and experiences in American culture and politics. By contrast, in Europe, the Anti-Defamation League's survey of anti-Semitism reports higher levels in all European countries surveyed, despite their having hate speech laws, than in the United States. A report from the EU Fundamental Rights Agency reports an increase in hate crimes between 2000 and 2009 in eleven out of fourteen surveyed EU nations. As one commentator puts it in his review of Waldron's discussion of hate speech, "Waldron demands that defenders of current First Amendment protections answer the question of whether the targets of abuse 'can [lead their lives], can their children be brought up, can their hopes be maintained and their worst fears dispelled, in a social environment polluted by [hate speech]?' The answer seems to be an emphatic 'yes.' "[85]

Finally, although advocates for speech codes claim that hate speech plays no part in the legitimate expression of ideas, we believe that censorship of words leads inevitably to the censorship of ideas. It is tempting to say that campuses should at the very least be able to prohibit epithets; words like "nigger" and "faggot" cause great harm. But it is not difficult to imagine contexts—in scholarly analysis, popular culture, or casual conversation—where the use of any given word would be considered appropriate. As Justice Harlan eloquently explained: "We cannot indulge the facile assumption that one can forbid particular words without also running a substantial risk of suppressing ideas in the process. Indeed, governments might soon seize upon the censorship of particular words as a convenient guise for banning the expression of unpopular views."[86] Hate speech codes inescapably ban the expression of unpopular ideas and views, which never is tolerable in colleges and universities.

But even if colleges and universities can't and shouldn't try to ban hate speech, they still must act to create a conducive learning environment for all students. The question becomes: what can they do?

CHAPTER FIVE

What Campuses Can and Can't Do

W E understand and often sympathize with those who want to punish hateful speech because they believe colleges and universities must take seriously their responsibility to maintain inclusive, nondiscriminatory learning environments. Those of us who believe in free speech values will not win over this generation of students by mocking them, calling them weak or coddled, or dismissing their legitimate concerns. They are correct to highlight the harmful impact of hateful or bullying speech, and correct that historically underrepresented groups face barriers to full inclusion within higher education. Free speech advocates must acknowledge the admirable values that tempt people toward censorship, and then provide a road map for addressing these issues in a way that does not undermine higher education's necessary commitment to free speech, academic freedom, unfettered inquiry, and robust debate. That is our goal in this chapter.

A major barrier to these efforts is that there is still much confusion about what free speech on college campuses actually means. Some students, hearing administrators talk about the value of free speech, will show up at campus events and shout down speakers they do not like, claiming that they are merely exercising their right to speak. Faculty members who claim the right to express themselves freely in public settings or on social media may argue that the same principles of freedom allow them to do whatever they want in their classrooms or prevent review of the quality of their scholarship. Campus efforts to nurture a voluntary culture of civility may encourage demands for mandatory trigger warnings on syllabi. The fact that universities prevent faculty and students from acting hatefully or uncivilly in professional academic settings leads to demands that administrators also punish people who are hateful or uncivil when protesting on campus. The freedom to protest on open campus grounds is used to claim a right to occupy campus buildings in a way that disrupts the campus's teaching mission or basic operation.

Some of these mistakes reflect a lack of information about basic free speech principles in the United States. Others are based on a failure to take into account the difference between general precepts of free speech, which apply without regard to the special teaching and research mission of college campuses, and the principles of academic freedom, which govern the expression of ideas within professional academic settings. Colleges and universities are properly expected to recognize

both a *professional zone*, which requires standards of peer review, scholarly norms, teaching excellence, and appropriate
conduct in the work environment, and a *free speech zone*, which
explicitly rejects professional educational standards in order
to allow for a more raucous space of expression, governed
only by the principles of the First Amendment.

We will describe, as specifically as we can, what should be
permissible and desirable, and impermissible and undesirable,
as universities deal with charges that certain forms of expression interfere with students' learning or make them feel unwelcome on campus. We offer this guidance as related pairs of
"can'ts" and "cans"—what campuses can and can't do to create inclusive learning environments. We realize, of course,
that the First Amendment restricts only government action,
so in a legal sense these guidelines apply only to public institutions. But as we have argued throughout, academic freedom
should be the same at public and private schools: the principles we describe should apply to both.[1]

> *A campus can't censor or punish speech merely because a*
> *person or group considers it offensive or hateful.*
> *A campus can censor or punish speech that meets the legal*
> *criteria for harassment, true threats, or other speech*
> *acts unprotected by the First Amendment.*

Colleges and universities can never punish the expression
of ideas. The very core of a university's mission requires protection of all views, no matter how objectionable or offensive
they may be to some students and faculty.

The Supreme Court has made clear that this is a basic
principle of the First Amendment. For example, in *Street v.*

New York (1969), the Court declared: "It is firmly settled that under our Constitution the public expression of ideas may not be prohibited merely because the ideas are themselves offensive to some of their hearers."[2] In *FCC v. Pacifica Foundation* (1978), the Court similarly explained: "The fact that society may find speech offensive is not a sufficient reason for suppressing it. Indeed, if it is the speaker's opinion that gives offense, that consequence is a reason for according it constitutional protection. For it is a central tenet of the First Amendment that the government must remain neutral in the marketplace of ideas."[3] In *Texas v. Johnson* (1989), the Court stated: "If there is a bedrock principle underlying the First Amendment, it is that the government may not prohibit the expression of an idea simply because society finds the idea itself offensive or disagreeable."[4] In *Boos v. Berry* (1988) it said: "In public debate [we] must tolerate insulting, and even outrageous, speech in order to provide adequate 'breathing space' to the freedoms protected by the First Amendment."[5]

More recently, in *Snyder v. Phelps* (2011), the Court made clear that speakers cannot be punished or held liable even for deeply offensive speech that causes great emotional distress.[6] For over twenty years, members of the Westboro Baptist Church have picketed military funerals to communicate their belief that God is punishing the United States for its tolerance of homosexuality, particularly in the military. Fred Phelps, who founded the church, and six Westboro Baptist parishioners (all relatives of his) traveled to Maryland to picket the funeral of Marine Lance Corporal Matthew Snyder, who was killed in Iraq in the line of duty. The picketing took place, in accordance with instructions from local law enforcement, on public land approximately one thousand feet from the church where the funeral was held. The picketers peacefully displayed signs reading "God Hates the USA/ Thank God for 9/11," "America is Doomed," "Don't Pray for the USA," "Thank God for IEDs," "Thank God for Dead Soldiers," "Pope in Hell," "Priests Rape Boys," "God Hates Fags," "You're Going to Hell," and "God Hates You."[7]

Albert Snyder, Matthew Snyder's father, saw the tops of the picketers' signs when driving to the funeral but did not learn what they said until he watched a news broadcast that night. He sued Phelps, Phelps's family members who were with him at the funeral, and the Westboro Baptist Church under Maryland state law, claiming intentional infliction of emotional distress, intrusion upon seclusion, and civil conspiracy. A jury in federal court ruled in Snyder's favor, and the district court judge allowed a $10 million judgment to stand. But the Supreme Court, with only Justice Samuel Alito dissenting, supported the rights of the protestors. As Chief Justice John Roberts explained, "Such speech cannot be restricted simply because it is upsetting or arouses contempt. Indeed, 'the point of all speech protection . . . is to shield just those choices of content that in someone's eyes are misguided, or even hurtful.' "[8] Roberts also emphasized that there cannot be liability for "intentional infliction of emotional distress" if the speech is protected by the First Amendment.

Still, we do not take the untenable position that freedom of speech is absolute. The Supreme Court has long recognized categories of unprotected and less-protected speech,[9] and these exceptions are crucial for colleges and universities. They must have the ability to prohibit true threats, harassment, destruction of property, and speech that disrupts classes or campus activities.[10]

True Threats

No one has a First Amendment right to cause another person to reasonably fear for his or her physical safety. The Supreme Court has held that "true threats" are not protected speech, a principle it first articulated in *Watts v. United States* (1969).[11] In that case, Robert Watts was heard to say, "If they ever make me carry a rifle the first man I want to get in my sights is LBJ [President Lyndon Johnson]. They are not going to make me kill my black brothers." He was convicted of violating a law that made it a crime to "knowingly and willfully . . . [threaten] to take the life of or to inflict bodily harm upon the President."[12] The Court ruled that the government must "prove a true 'threat.' We do not believe that the kind of political hyperbole indulged in by petitioner fits within that statutory term."[13] The Court elaborated on the meaning of "true threat" in *Virginia v. Black* (2003), explaining that " 'true threats' encompass those statements when the speaker means to communicate a serious intent to commit an act of unlawful violence to a particular individual or group of individuals. The speaker need not actually intend to carry out the threat."[14]

On college campuses, speech should be subject to punishment if it causes a reasonable person to fear for his or her safety. True threats fall outside the protections of the First Amendment because a prohibition on such speech "protects individuals from the fear of violence" and "from the disruption that fear engenders," in addition to protecting people "from the possibility that the threatened violence will occur."[15]

The assessment is based on a "reasonable person" standard, not on the subjective view of any concerned person, because otherwise campuses will be back in the position of having to censor or punish speech merely because an especially sensitive or fearful person claims to feel threatened by the expression of ideas he or she does not like. In the context of a campus environment, the definition of "true threat" can focus on how a reasonable *student* would interpret the speech.

While we recognize the inherent difficulty of applying any "reasonable person" standard, it has proven to be workable for determining when speech can be punished. For example, the United States Court of Appeals for the Ninth Circuit used that standard to conclude that an anti-abortion website constituted a true threat against doctors who were featured in "wanted posters" that included their home addresses and personal information and said they were "wanted for crimes against humanity," especially after other doctors who had been similarly depicted had been murdered.[16] The court explained that "a reasonable person would foresee that the listener will believe he will be subjected to physical violence upon his person"; thus the speech was "unprotected by the First Amendment."[17]

Preventing "true threats" focuses on protecting a person from fear of physical harm, but not from emotional injury. We believe this distinction is essential. If emotional harm were enough to justify suppression or punishment of speech, any view or idea that caused emotional distress could be stopped. We do not discount the importance of emotional injuries, but we see no way to allow liability for emotional harms without also allowing restrictions on the expression of ideas and views.

Harassment

Freedom of speech does not protect a right to harass an individual on account of his or her race, sex, religion, or sexual orientation. What is the line between permissible speech and impermissible harassment? The mere presence of offensive speech cannot be enough for harassment, but there is no free speech right to subject a person to repeated, directed actions that interfere with his or her education.

The law of harassment developed under Title VII of the 1964 Civil Rights Act, which prohibits employers from "discriminat[ing] against any individual with respect to his . . . conditions or privileges of employment because of such individual's race, color, religion, sex or national origin." At the urging of scholars such as Catharine MacKinnon, the Supreme Court recognized workplace harassment as a form of discrimination prohibited by Title VII.[18] MacKinnon argued that there are two basic types of sexual harassment: quid pro quo harassment, such as when an employer says, "sleep with me or you're fired," and a hostile, intimidating or offensive workplace.

While the first category, quid pro quo harassment, poses no problems under the First Amendment, the second category raises difficult free speech questions.[19] Nevertheless, the Supreme Court has adopted this framework and found that sexual harassment in the workplace violates Title VII.[20] In recent decades, courts and administrative agencies have clarified the boundaries between free speech and harassment. Regulations adopted by the Equal Employment Opportunity Commission (EEOC) identify five elements that must be met for a claim of hostile workplace harassment:

- verbal or physical conduct of a sexual or sex-based nature;
- the conduct is unwelcome;
- the conduct is directed against an individual because of her (or his) sex;
- the conduct has the purpose or effect of unreasonably interfering with an individual's work performance or creating an intimidating, hostile, or offensive working environment;
- the employer knew or should have known of the conduct and did not take adequate action to stop or prevent it.[21]

Title IX of the Education Amendments of 1972 prohibits educational institutions receiving federal funds from discriminating on the basis of sex,[22] and the Department of Education has created regulations and interpretive guidelines that are similar to the ones put forward by the EEOC.[23] In *Franklin v. Gwinnett County Public Schools*, the Supreme Court unanimously ruled that a student has the same right to sue for sexual harassment under Title IX that an employee has under Title VII.[24] Title VI of the 1964 Civil Rights Act prohibits recipients of federal funds, including universities, from discriminating based on race, and race-based harassment is subject to the same five-part test.

These legal developments have made campuses fully obligated to comply with the anti-harassment components of federal anti-discrimination law, which include training requirements, reporting requirements, the establishment of effective grievance procedures, taking immediate and appropriate action when an employee complains, and protecting those who file discrimination charges from retaliation. There is also well-settled case law on the circumstances under which campuses are expected to take affirmative steps to learn about discriminatory conditions, so that they cannot later claim ignorance. These requirements—which extend to both the workplace and the learning environment—often go unnoticed outside the campus administration. Individual instances of offensive speech draw far more attention than the daily efforts to satisfy the requirements of federal anti-discrimination law. But the constant attention to ensuring compliance with federal law is crucial in creating a positive culture of nondiscrimination.

The Foundation for Individual Rights in Education has explained that "discriminatory harassment, properly understood and as defined by the Supreme Court, refers to conduct that is (1) unwelcome; (2) discriminatory; (3) on the basis of gender or another protected status, like race; (4) directed at an individual; and (5) 'so severe, pervasive, and objectively offensive, and that so undermines and detracts from the victims' educational experience, that the victim-students are effectively denied equal access to an institution's resources and opportunities.' "[25] As one commentator wrote, speech must "meet a threshold of severity or pervasiveness that would objectively prevent an individual from participating in educational programs."[26] Speech that merely expresses offensive views toward a protected class or is rude, discourteous, or "simple teasing" does not rise to the level of adversely affecting a student's educational opportunities and benefits.[27]

Under this approach, a noose placed on a tree on a campus cannot by itself be deemed harassment, but a noose tacked to an African American student's door in a dormitory could be regarded as harassment (or a true threat) unprotected by the First Amendment. Singing a highly offensive racist song on a bus, as occurred at the University of Oklahoma, is protected by the First Amendment, but repeatedly yelling racist epithets at minority students on campus is not. Saying hateful things to a general audience in a public place is protected, but a person who adds African American students to a group text message with racially charged images and threats of lynching can be punished because this targeted act can be reasonably interpreted as representing harassment or a true threat of harm to particular people.[28] Posting an anti-Asian rant on YouTube cannot be punished, but targeting Asian students with repeated harassing emails can be.

These principles call into question a recent decision of the University of Oregon to treat offensive expression by a professor as discriminatory harassment. In October 2016, the University of Oregon Law School suspended Nancy Shurtz, a law professor, after she wore blackface and a hospital gown at a Halloween party. She said that she was doing so to promote a conversation about race, inspired by her admiration for Dr. Damon Tweedy's book *Black Man in a White Coat*. Twenty-three law school faculty members wrote a letter urging the professor to resign. The University of Oregon commissioned an investigation which found that her costume exacerbated racial tensions on campus in a way that had a disproportionate impact on students of color, because "minority students [felt] they have become burdened with educating other students about racial issues and racial sensitivity" and because some students used "other offensive racially based terminology during class times in the context of discussing this event and broader racial issues." The report concluded: "We find that Nancy Shurtz's costume . . . constitutes a violation of the university's policies against discrimination. We further find that the actions constitute discriminatory harassment."[29]

We, of course, understand why students and faculty were offended by the professor's actions, and it is clear that the campus was roiled by the ensuing sense of outrage. But it is deeply troubling to use the law of harassment as the basis for finding that her speech was unprotected and that she could be sanctioned for her actions. From the vantage point of ensuring a culture of free expression, there is no difference between sanctioning faculty members because administrators or donors object to their views and sanctioning them because many students are outraged or have been made uncomfortable by the subsequent conversations that arose as a result of otherwise protected speech. Either justification creates boundless opportunities to fire professors for expressing unpopular opinions or ideas.[30] Being very upset that a faculty member or student said something hateful, offensive, or ignorant cannot transform protected speech into harassment without fatally undermining free speech protections. Any other approach risks punishment for any speech that enough members of the academic community refuse to tolerate.

Similarly, anti-discrimination obligations under Title VI and Title IX should never lead campuses to investigate a person merely because a member of the university community is offended by his or her expression of a view. Before any steps are taken by a university, the complaining party should be required to identify a pattern of discriminatory conduct that falls within the legal definitions of harassment.

We make this point because there is reason to be deeply concerned about how the Department of Education's Office of Civil Rights (OCR) is interpreting obligations on campuses, and whether it is forcing campuses to violate free speech guarantees. A months-long investigation of professor Laura Kipnis should not have been triggered by her publishing an article in a scholarly journal. The OCR should not have instructed the University of New Mexico to punish unwelcome "verbal conduct" of a sexual nature that did not amount to harassment. In light of these occurrences, the OCR should immediately clarify that campuses will not be at risk under Title VI or Title IX for failing to restrict or punish protected speech, and it should update its guidelines to ensure that no investigations by campuses or by OCR can be triggered merely by an allegation that someone was upset by the expression of ideas or views.

Destruction of Property

There is, of course, no First Amendment right to destroy someone else's property, even if it is done to communicate a message. Colleges and universities can punish such conduct.

Disruption of Classes and Campus Activities

There is no First Amendment right to disrupt classes or other campus activities. This is a corollary of the long-established principle that there is no right to speak in ways that constitute an actual breach of the peace. A person has a general right to express a point of view, but not with a bullhorn outside someone's house in the middle of the night. People have a right to decry what is happening at a judicial proceeding, but not to go into a courtroom and shout during those proceedings. People have a right to have their say, but not in a way that prevents others from going about their legitimate business. The key is that any restrictions must be content-neutral and must apply to disruptive speech regardless of its subject or viewpoint.

This limit on speech is illustrated by an incident on our campus some years go. On February 8, 2010, Israeli ambassador Michael Oren spoke at an event at the University of California, Irvine, at the invitation of several schools and groups on campus. As he began to speak, a student from the audience shouted so that Ambassador Oren could not be heard. The disruptive student was removed and Oren again began to speak, only for another student to shout so that Oren again could not be heard. This happened eleven times with eleven different students; each student was removed, and ultimately Oren was able to speak.

The students claimed that their speech was protected by the First Amendment, but this claim was ultimately rejected by the courts. The protestors could have held their own event or picketed or distributed leaflets, but disrupting a speaker is not conduct protected by the First Amendment. Campuses can and should prevent or punish disruptive efforts designed to deny others their free speech rights. As expressed in the Statement on Principles of Free Expression at the University of Chicago, written by professor Geoffrey Stone, "Although faculty, students and staff are free to criticize, contest and condemn the views expressed on campus, they may not obstruct, disrupt, or otherwise interfere with the freedom of others to express views they reject or even loathe."[31]

Likewise, there is not a First Amendment right to occupy campus buildings, block access to them, or otherwise interfere with normal university functions. To say that these activities are not protected by free speech principles does not mean that they always should be punished. There are certainly instances where it seems wiser to allow the students to temporarily disrupt an event, or occupy a building or offices within it, in the hope of avoiding the ill will engendered by a show of force. But that kind of accommodation is entirely discretionary and based on practical considerations rather than principles of free speech. It is especially important to avoid such accommodations when the goal of protestors is to interfere with others on campus who are exercising their rights. Allowing short-term protest activity in the lobby of an administrative building is less a threat to free speech values than allowing disruptions of unpopular speakers or the expression of ideas in educational settings. Campuses should be especially vigilant to prevent those sorts of disruptions or to respond to them as serious violations of campus codes of conduct.

A campus can't prevent protestors from having a meaningful opportunity to get their views across in an effective way.

A campus can impose time, place, and manner restrictions on protests for the purpose of preventing protestors from disrupting the normal work of the campus,

*including the educational environment and adminis-
trative operations.*

The Berkeley Free Speech Movement established the principle that students and faculty have the right to express themselves on a broad range of topics, and have the right to use campus grounds for personal and political expression. Campuses thus must make efforts to accommodate this expression in ways that make it meaningful and that allow members of the campus community to find an audience. Campuses cannot separate protestors from all potential audiences by restricting them to marginal areas.

Yet it has been a long-standing aspect of First Amendment law that communities can impose reasonable "time, place, and manner" restrictions on expression. This phrase refers to government's ability to regulate speech in a public forum—government property that it is required to make available for speech—in a manner that minimizes disruption of a public place while still protecting free speech. You have a right to protest, but not to block the freeway. You can use a bullhorn in a public park, but not in a public library. In some locations, what you are allowed to say in public at noon perhaps may not be said at midnight. You can hold up placards or signs, unless your doing so would block the views of the people behind you. As a rule, the Court has approved reasonable time, place, and manner restrictions "provided that they are justified without reference to the content of the regulated speech, that they serve a significant governmental interest, and that in doing so they leave open ample alternative channels for communication of the information."[32]

In *Heffron v. International Society for Krishna Consciousness, Inc.* (1981), for example, the Supreme Court upheld a regulation at the Minnesota State Fair that prohibited the distribution of literature or the soliciting of funds except at booths, which were available on a first-come, first-serve basis.[33] The International Society for Krishna Consciousness wanted its members to do these things while walking the fairgrounds, and it argued that that the regulation violated its religious freedom. The Court said that the regulation was content-neutral because it applied to all literature and solicitations, regardless of the speaker, viewpoint, or subject matter, and was a reasonable way of regulating the flow of pedestrian traffic through the state fairgrounds.[34] The Court also observed that the Krishna group had other ways of reaching its audience: its members could walk around outside the fairgrounds, or they could obtain a booth.

Many other time, place, and manner restrictions have also been upheld. In *Kovacs v. Cooper* (1949), the Court upheld a restriction on the use of sound amplification devices such as loudspeakers on trucks.[35] In *Grayned v. Rockford* (1972) it upheld a city ordinance that prohibited any "person, while on public or private grounds adjacent to any building in which a school or any class thereof is in session, [from making] any noise or diversion which disturbs or tends to disturb the peace or good order of such school."[36] The Court said that the "crucial question is whether the manner of expression is basically incompatible with the normal activity of a particular place at a particular time."[37]

Time, place, and manner restrictions apply on college campuses as well. Campuses can designate certain areas as speech zones and restrict speech in other areas, so long as the rules are not based on the content of the speech and the zones are not so restrictive as to prevent speakers from having a meaningful opportunity to get their views across. For example, campuses cannot use time, place, and manner regulations to restrict students to one small designated free speech zone that can only be used with prior permission between 9 a.m. and 4 p.m., and exclude any free speech on public sidewalks, walkways, lawns, and other outdoor areas.[38] However, campuses can limit speech activities in and near classroom buildings while classes are in session to prevent disruption of class activities. Schools can condition the use of special facilities on requirements that apply to all, such as limits on occupancy or proof that outside security officials are properly bonded and insured. They may deny requests for gatherings that present insurmountable logistical or security challenges, or if accommodating such challenges would impose costs above a generally applied threshold. More broadly, they can prohibit the disruption of speakers or other campus activities, such as commencement, and can restrict or punish individuals who attempt disruption.

> *A campus can't impose content-based speech restrictions in dormitories.*
> *A campus can impose content-neutral restrictions in dormitories designed to ensure a supportive living environment for students.*

The concept of time, place, and manner restrictions has special significance for college dormitories. It is crucial that campuses protect dormitories as spaces where students can find repose. Therefore, they are places where speech can be restricted, so long as the restrictions are not based on the views expressed. The Supreme Court already has recognized this for speech around people's homes. In *Frisby v. Schultz* (1988), the Court sustained an ordinance that prohibited picketing "before or about" any residence.[39] Although it was adopted in response to targeted picketing of a doctor's home by antiabortion protestors, the Court concluded that the law was permissible because it was content neutral and was narrowly tailored to protect people's tranquility and repose in their homes. Justice O'Connor wrote for the Court, "The First Amendment permits the government to prohibit offensive speech as intrusive when the 'captive' audience cannot avoid the objectionable speech. . . . The resident is figuratively, and perhaps literally, trapped within the home."[40] Colleges and universities can and should apply this standard to speech in dormitories. Students in dormitories, too, are captive audiences.

But even regulations meant to protect a captive audience cannot be based on the ideas espoused. What is placed on walls or bulletin boards or in dormitory windows may be regulated so long as the rules are content neutral and applied in a content-neutral manner. A campus may choose to keep students from putting bulletin boards on their doors or displays in their windows, but universities cannot target and exclude certain views and not others. For instance, a campus could have a rule preventing students from affixing anything to the windows of their dormitory rooms, but a campus could not prohibit just the display of Confederate flags on dormitory windows.

A campus can't censor or punish some speakers, but not others, for putting up handbills, writing messages in chalk, or engaging in similar acts of expression.

A campus can create general content-neutral regulations governing on-campus expression.

There must be places on campus available for speech, even if providing them imposes some costs on the university. *Hague v. CIO*[41] and *Schneider v. State of New Jersey*,[42] both decided in 1939, were crucial in recognizing this right. *Hague* involved an attempt by a mayor to prevent a union, the Congress of Industrial Organizations, from organizing in his city. An ordinance was enacted that prohibited all public meetings in the streets and other public places without a city permit. In a famous plurality opinion, Justice Owen Roberts found that there was a right to use government property for speech purposes. Roberts wrote: "Wherever the title of streets and parks may rest, they have immemorially been held in trust for the use of the public and, time out of mind, have been used for purposes of assembly, communicating thought between citizens, and discussing public questions. Such use of the streets and public places has, from ancient times, been a part of the privileges, immunities, rights, and liberties of citizens."[43]

In *Schneider*, the Court struck down a city ordinance that prohibited the distribution of leaflets on public property. The city of Irvington, New Jersey, maintained that it could do so to minimize litter and maintain the appearance of its streets. The Court rejected this argument. In another opinion by Justice Roberts, the Court said: "We are of opinion that the purpose to keep the streets clean and of good appearance is insufficient to justify an ordinance which prohibits a person rightfully on a public street from handing literature to one willing to receive it. Any burden imposed upon the city authorities in cleaning and caring for the streets as an indirect consequence of such distribution results from the constitutional protection of the freedom of speech and press."[44] *Schneider* is important because it established that a city must allow speech on its property even if doing so will impose costs on the city,[45] especially because "the streets are natural and proper places for the dissemination of information and opinion; and one is not to have the exercise of his liberty of expression in appropriate places abridged on the plea that it may be exercised in some other place."[46]

People thus have a right to hand out leaflets on campus or write on the sidewalk in chalk, even though this will impose costs for cleaning up on the university. But campuses can have content-neutral rules, such as time, place, and manner restrictions. If a campus permits chalking, it could say that chalking has to be on outdoor sidewalks that are open to the rain, not on the sides of buildings, and it may prohibit spray paint. A school could say that leaflets can be distributed in public areas of the campus, but not placed under the doors of students' dorm rooms. Such rules are permissible because they apply to all expression and serve obvious important interests.

A campus can't engage in content-based discrimination against faculty, students, or other speakers or writers who seek to express themselves outside the professional educational context.

A campus can engage in content-based evaluation of faculty and students who are operating within the professional educational context, as long as this evaluation is based on professional standards or peer assessments of the quality of scholarship or teaching.

We are disturbed that some campuses have recently excluded speakers with controversial viewpoints, or ruled that an invited speaker will not be allowed unless there is a competing perspective at the event. Campuses must be open to all ideas and views, no matter how controversial or even offensive, and outside of the educational context they cannot mandate the creation of a balanced or impartial program. In the free speech zone, speakers or groups are allowed to have their say on their terms. Of course, a campus can't prevent students from expressing their disagreement with invited speakers or other campus activities; in fact, they should work to create a culture that welcomes controversial speech and encourages opponents to engage and rebut it rather than try to suppress it.

For faculty, freedom of speech is essential to the exercise of academic freedom. This was eloquently expressed by the Supreme Court in *Sweezy v. New Hampshire* (1957), where the Court found unconstitutional a college professor's conviction for contempt because he refused to answer questions about his political beliefs.[47] Chief Justice Earl Warren wrote for the Court:

Academic freedom and political expression [are] areas in which government should be extremely reticent to tread. The essentiality of freedom in the community of American universities is almost self-evident. No one should underestimate the vital role in a democracy that is played by those who guide and train our youth. To impose any strait jacket upon the intellectual leaders in our colleges and universities would imperil the future of our Nation. No field of education is so thoroughly comprehended by man that new discoveries cannot yet be made. Particularly is that true in the social sciences, where few, if any, principles are accepted as absolutes. Scholarship cannot flourish in an atmosphere of suspicion and distrust. Teachers and students must always remain free to inquire, to study and to evaluate, to gain new maturity and understanding; otherwise our civilization will stagnate and die.[48]

It follows that that faculty members at public universities must be accorded First Amendment protection that the Supreme Court has denied to other government employees. In *Garcetti v. Ceballos*, the Court held that there is no First Amendment protection for the speech of government employees on the job in the scope of their duties. The case involved Richard Ceballos, a supervising district attorney in Los Angeles County who concluded that a witness in one of his cases, a deputy sheriff, was not telling the truth.[49] He wrote a memo to this effect and felt that he was required by the Constitution to inform the defense of this. As a result of this speech, Ceballos alleged that his employers retaliated against him, transferring him to a less desirable position and denying him a promotion. Although the Supreme Court long has held that the speech of government employees is constitutionally protected,[50] it ruled against Ceballos. The Court drew a distinction between speech "as a citizen" and speech "as a public employee," and said only the former is protected by the First Amendment.[51] The Court expressed great concern about the disruptive effects of allowing employees to bring First Amendment claims based on on-the-job speech.

As applied to public colleges and universities, *Garcetti v. Ceballos* (2006) would mean that professors have no First Amendment protection for their scholarly writing or teaching because it is speech on the job and within the scope of their duties. Justice David Souter, in dissent, stressed his concern for what this would mean for academic freedom[52] and the Court acknowledged that academic freedom could pose a different issue that it was not addressing.[53] The Ninth Circuit subsequently reached exactly this conclusion: "We conclude that *Garcetti* does not—indeed, consistent with the First Amendment, cannot—apply to teaching and academic writing that are performed 'pursuant to the official duties' of a teacher and professor."[54] This is an essential clarification of how *Garcetti* should apply in settings that implicate the values of academic freedom.

But the First Amendment and principles of freedom of expression do not preclude campus evaluation of the professional quality of teaching or scholarship, nor do they preclude the campus from requiring that faculty members be fair-minded when presenting materials in educational settings. Neither free speech principles nor academic freedom gives a faculty member the right to use the classroom as his or her personal platform for the expression of political opinions without regard to professional norms, or to prevent students from having their fair opportunity to express views without fear of being punished.

This principle was reiterated by the University of California in 2003 after a controversy over a course description by a pro-Palestinian basic writing instructor at Berkeley.[55] Entitled "The Politics and Poetics of Palestinian Resistance," the description referred to "the brutal Israeli military occupation of Palestine" and warned that "conservative thinkers are encouraged to seek [another] section." After a media firestorm, University of California president Richard Atkinson asked Berkeley law professor Robert Post (later the dean at Yale Law School) to examine the issues of academic freedom that the controversy raised.

In his report, Post noted that it would not be proper to criticize the course on grounds of offensiveness, because "robust scholarly dialogue . . . can be fierce, consequential, and hurtful to those who care intently about their ideals."[56] Rather, the key question was "whether the course description complies with relevant professional standards," and while faculty may be permitted to convey to students that course material will be approached from a certain perspective, that is different from "using a course description as a platform for political preaching. It is possible that the rhetoric of a course description can become so excessive as to become a political tract that bears little relationship to the pedagogical justification of disclosure [of personal perspective]. Faculty members have no business using course descriptions for the mere purpose of disseminating their political views."[57] While "there is no academic norm that prohibits scholarship from communicating definite viewpoints about important and controversial issues," the faculty must also recognize "the academic freedom of students," including their "right to think freely and to exercise independent judgment."[58] The debate led the university to revise its statement of academic freedom to clarify professors' right to express themselves in class with passion, but also to note their obligations to be judged by professional standards and to defend the rights of their students.

Faculty members may choose to provide students warnings before presenting material that might be offensive or upsetting to them.

Colleges and universities should not impose requirements that faculty provide "trigger warnings" before presenting or assigning material that might be offensive or upsetting to students.

Recently, many campuses have considered requiring faculty members to post warnings on syllabi and course materials if some students might find the course content emotionally disturbing.[59] In February 2014, student leaders at the University of California, Santa Barbara, passed a resolution encouraging professors to include trigger warnings in the syllabi for courses that contain potentially upsetting content. The resolution also urged professors of any such course to "not . . . dock points from a student's overall grade for being absent or leaving class early if the reason for the absence is the triggering content."[60] A guide distributed to professors at Oberlin College instructed them: "Triggers are not only relevant to sexual misconduct, but also to anything that might cause trauma. Be aware of racism, classism, sexism, heterosexism, cissexism, ableism, and other issues of privilege or oppression."[61]

Warning students before exposing them to offensive or upsetting material is nothing new. Before we read our students the racist chant from the fraternity at the University of Oklahoma, we cautioned them that it was racist and deeply offensive. Long before anyone coined the phrase "trigger warnings," we would warn students when we were coming to material that might be offensive, such as in playing for them George Carlin's monologue on the "seven dirty words" when studying the Supreme Court decision about it.[62]

Trigger warnings might be seen as "more speech," since they use speech—the warnings—to prepare students for exposure to offensive material. They also show that the professor is sensitive to the difficulty in dealing with the material.[63] We thus reject the view that all trigger warnings are to be condemned as "coddling of students."[64]

Still, although we do not object such warnings, it is wrong for universities to require them. Professors need to decide how to best educate their students, and for some faculty members, this might include a professional judgment that being exposed to material without a warning makes for more effective instruction. Requiring trigger warnings might cause some professors to change their course assignments and course coverage.[65] It also may force professors to characterize their material in a way that does not reflect their views of the material or the appropriate response to it. Labels warning students that a book's themes are racist or sexist may bias students' reactions in a way that faculty members consider wrong or unfair, and would cast the same pall of censorship that would exist if college librarians were required to add warning labels to the front of selected library books. Although trigger warnings are often desirable, we agree with the Committee on Academic Freedom for the AAUP, which declared, "Institutional requirements or even suggestions that faculty use trigger warnings interfere with faculty academic freedom in the choice of course materials and teaching methods."[66]

Campuses can create "safe spaces" in educational settings
that ensure that individuals feel free to express the
widest array of viewpoints, and can support student
efforts to self-organize in ways that reflect shared inter-
ests and experiences.

Campuses can't use the concept of "safe spaces" to censor the
expression of ideas considered too offensive for students
to hear.

The phrase "safe spaces" has been applied to many different activities on campuses. The concept can be used in ways
that enhance free speech and in ways that undermine it.[67] For
example, it is appropriate—and even necessary—for campuses
and professors to do all they can to make sure that the classroom is a safe space for scholarly exploration, civil debate,
reasoned discussion, and making mistakes. The best educational environments remove fears that students may have
about asking certain questions or challenging prevailing ex-
planations; the worst environments are those where students
feel that they can be punished for expressing views that the
professor or other classmates consider heretical. A classroom
should be a place where antiracism advocates can ask about
the role of race in the choice of course materials, conserva-
tives can question the wisdom or constitutionality of affirmative action, and socialists can criticize the dominant position
of the concept of efficiency in economic models. It is a good
thing when the idea of a "safe space" refers to a place where
one feels safe to *express* an opinion, without punishment, harassing judgment, or bullying condemnation. It is the theme
of this book that campuses must be safe spaces in this sense.

The concept is also used to refer to efforts by students to exercise their rights of association and create places on campus where they are with people who are like-minded or who share certain experiences. Campuses have always had student societies, fraternities and sororities, student government groups, chess clubs, band rooms, gatherings of College Republicans and College Democrats, theater groups, Christian clubs, Hillel and Chabad, and countless other associations that allow members of a diverse student body to find their place. It raised no concerns in earlier years and should raise no concerns today when its advocates are underrepresented minority students or the LGBTQ community. In fact, if campuses prevented such ordinary activity they would be limiting the associational rights of students in violation of free speech principles.

However, the concept of safe spaces also has been used as a basis for demanding that campuses protect students from being exposed to disagreeable or offensive ideas. This is the "safe space activism" underlying the "no platform" movement among students in the UK,[68] and also underlies much of the rhetoric used by some student groups who demand that American campuses remove all hateful or offensive speech. At Emory University, after Trump supporters chalked "Trump" on sidewalks, one protestor complained, "I'm supposed to feel comfortable and safe [here]. . . . I don't deserve to feel afraid at my school."[69] When Wesleyan University's newspaper, the *Argus*, published an opinion essay that criticized the Black Lives Matter Movement, critics pushed to defund the newspaper on the grounds that publishing such an essay "neglects to provide a safe space for the voices of students of color."[70] When conservative commentator Ben Shapiro spoke at the University of Wisconsin on the topic of "Dismantling Safe Spaces: Facts Don't Care About Your Feelings," protestors declared Shapiro's mere presence on the campus as a threat to the sense of safety and "personal violences" of many students, and interrupted the speech with repeated shouts of "safety!"[71] Campuses cannot and should not accommodate the language of safe spaces when the focus is protecting members of the campus *from* the expression of ideas, rather than creating a safe environment *for* the expression of ideas.

> *A campus can't prohibit students or faculty from using words that some consider to be examples of "microaggressions."*
>
> *A campus can sensitize students and faculty to the impact that certain words may have, as part of an effort to create a respectful work and learning environment.*

The concept of microaggressions is now much discussed. As one commentator observed: "The term 'microaggression' was used by Columbia professor Derald Sue to refer to 'brief and commonplace daily verbal, behavioral, or environmental indignities, whether intentional or unintentional, that communicate hostile, derogatory, or negative racial slights and insults toward people of color.' Sue borrowed the term from psychiatrist Dr. Chester Pierce who coined the term in the '70s."[72]

In most current debates, the word "microaggression" refers to a very familiar idea: sometimes, even if we do not intend it, our everyday language is disrespectful to others. The language commonly used in society and in the workplace has changed dramatically for the better over the years. The "honeypies" or "darlings" that might have been prevalent in the office during the age of Mad Men are happily less prevalent. It should embarrass all people of goodwill to remember what the dominant culture thought was permissible to say, in polite company, about racial, ethnic, and religious minorities, or what used to be considered funny. At each moment of progress it has also been common to hear people grumble that the complaining groups are too sensitive or are engaging in annoying gestures of political correctness.

To the extent that current debates about microaggressions are an extension of this ordinary social evolution, the topic raises no free speech issues. Campuses should try to sensitize their communities to the kinds of words and statements that might be unintentionally offensive. We should all listen when others tell us they feel insulted and hurt. If the changes in language that campuses occasionally suggest seem unnecessary or too extreme, that can be debated or criticized. Campuses should also take steps—through formal training and other initiatives—to sensitize the community about the insidious effects of implicit bias.

A problem arises only when there are efforts to force campuses to police and punish such expression. Outside the legal limits on harassment and other unprotected activities, campuses are not permitted to do this. The occasional use of a phrase that some people find offensive cannot be the basis for censorship or punishment. There is an enormous difference between advocating norms of civility in expression—which always exist and which we all are taught from a young age— and enforcing these norms by censorship or punishment.

Microaggressions are an example of how a false dichotomy is often drawn between campuses punishing speech or their doing nothing. There is a middle course of campuses working to educate students as to situations where their words can cause harm, often unknowingly.

> *A campus can ensure that all student organizations, as a condition for recognition and receipt of funding, be open to all students, and can impose sanctions on student organizations for conduct if it is not protected by principles of freedom of speech.*
>
> *A campus cannot deny recognition to a student organization or impose sanctions against it for the views or ideas expressed by the organization, its members, or its speakers.*

In *Christian Legal Society v. Martinez* (2010), the Supreme Court upheld the University of California, Hastings College of Law's policy that required that "Registered Student Organizations" (RSOs) accept "all-comers" and prohibited discrimination based on characteristics such as race, sex, religion, disability, or sexual orientation.[73] The Christian Legal Society at Hastings Law School required its members to sign a "Statement of Faith" which affirmed a belief in Jesus Christ as their savior; the Society also excluded "unrepentant homosexuals" from membership.[74] Hastings refused to recognize the Christian Legal Society as an RSO, which meant that it could not get student activity funds or officially reserve school facilities for its use. The Supreme Court, ruling in favor of Hastings, explained that "the open-access policy ensures that the leadership, educational, and social opportunities afforded by [RSOs] are available to all students,"[75] "encourages tolerance, cooperation, and learning among students," and "incorporates—in fact, subsumes—state-law proscriptions on discrimination."[76] The Court found that the policy was, by definition, viewpoint neutral.

We share the Supreme Court's view that officially recognized student organizations should be open to all students. Moreover, student organizations should not be subject to punishment, such as denial of recognition or of funding, for the views they express or those conveyed by their members or speakers. But, of course, organizations may be sanctioned for conduct that is not protected speech and they can be punished if their membership rules violate antidiscrimination laws and rules. A student organization that plans a disruption of a school activity or systematically harasses other students can be punished, just as individual students who engage in such conduct can be punished.

> *Colleges and universities can punish speech over the internet and social media that otherwise is not protected, such as true threats and harassment or speech inconsistent with professional standards.*
> *Colleges and universities can't punish speech over the internet on the ground that it is offensive.*

Throughout this chapter, we have deliberately drawn no distinction based on the medium used for speech. There is no reason for campuses to treat speech differently based on whether it is transmitted through old means or new. We recognize, of course, that the internet and social media make it possible for harmful speech to reach a large audience very quickly. But the principles of free speech do not change.

Speech on the internet and social media cannot be prohibited or punished on the ground that it is offensive, even deeply offensive; colleges and universities may punish threats or harassment that occur via these media; and campuses and their officials can and should respond with more speech when appropriate.

Nor does it matter that speech on the internet and social media are not in any particular location. Some people argue that because the internet and social media are "off campus," colleges and universities may not impose discipline for speech that occurs via these media.[77] We reject this position. If a student's speech over social media constitutes a true threat or meets the test for harassment of another student or faculty member, it is not protected by the First Amendment. The expression is what causes the harm; its physical location is incidental.

Others have suggested that campuses be limited to regulating speech over social media that relates to the academic program of the university. Jeffrey Sun, Neal Hutchens, and James Breslin, for example, argue: "With speech occurring outside of an instructional setting, . . . a sufficient curricular nexus should exist . . . to subject student speech to institutional authority on academic grounds."[78] There is no doubt that colleges and universities can discipline a student's online speech if it relates directly to his or her academic program.[79] For example, in *Tatro v. University of Minnesota*, the Minnesota Supreme Court upheld sanctions imposed on a student, including a failing grade in a course, for her postings on Facebook.[80] The student was taking a mortuary science program; the course syllabus for her anatomy lab included rules "set up to promote respect for the cadaver." These rules allowed "respectful and discreet" "conversational language of cadaver dissection outside the laboratory" but prohibited "blogging" about the anatomy lab or cadaver dissection.[81] The student made repeated Facebook postings, some of which were about her cadaver, that she described as "satirical commentary and violent fantasy about her school experience."[82] The Minnesota Supreme Court upheld the discipline, concluding "that the University did not violate the free speech rights of [the student] by imposing sanctions for her Facebook posts that violated academic program rules where the academic program rules were narrowly tailored and directly related to established professional conduct standards."[83]

Colleges and universities also have an affirmative duty to try to ensure that students and other community members do not use the internet to convey true threats or harassment of other students. The Supreme Court has clearly ruled that an educational institution can be held liable if it is "deliberately indifferent" to harassment of its students.[84] There thus may be times when a school administrator will need to ask social media to remove threatening or harassing speech, or take other action to protect students.[85]

A campus should expect university administrators to speak out against especially egregious speech acts and, most important, encourage the university community to make its own decisions about what speech acts deserve praise or condemnation.

A campus should not expect university administrators to comment on or condemn every campus speech act that some person considers offensive.

Long ago, Justice Louis Brandeis, in one of the Supreme Court's most eloquent defenses of freedom of speech, said that the best remedy for speech we dislike is more speech. He wrote that the "fitting remedy for evil counsels is good ones" and that "if there be time to expose through discussion the falsehood and fallacies, to avert the evil by the processes of education, the remedy to be applied is more speech, not enforced silence."[86] Again, Geoffrey Stone's Statement on Principles of Freedom of Expression at the University of Chicago captures this well: "For members of the University community, as for the University itself, the proper response to ideas they find offensive, unwarranted and dangerous is not interference, obstruction, or suppression. It is, instead, to engage in robust counter-speech that challenges the merits of those ideas and exposes them for what they are. To this end, the University has a solemn responsibility not only to promote a lively and fearless freedom of debate and deliberation, but also to protect that freedom when others attempt to restrict it. As Robert M. Hutchins observed, without a vibrant commitment to free and open inquiry, a university ceases to be a university."[87]

One of the most powerful tools that campuses and their officials possess—and one too often overlooked—is the ability to speak. This can take many forms. Colleges should have principles of community expressing what they expect of students. These principles can stress the importance of an inclusive learning environment and can declare that speech expressing hate on the basis of race, sex, religion, or sexual orientation is inconsistent with the values of the campus. Campuses should ensure that the academic community pays serious attention to issues relating to the harms associated with intolerance and structural discrimination. There should be robust efforts to organize co-curricular activities that celebrate cultural diversity and give victims of hateful and bullying acts the opportunity to have their voices heard. Campuses should emphasize that creating and transmitting new knowledge is best accomplished when people of diverse backgrounds and perspectives work together in an environment of respectful engagement.

And it must be remembered that campus officials and other members of the campus community also have free speech rights, and they can and should condemn hate speech when it occurs and explain why it is inimical to the desired community. There are many instances where members of the campus community have done exactly this to great success. At Bowie State University, for instance, a swastika was painted on a column on the patio of the Martin Luther King Jr. Communication Arts Center. Campus officials immediately declared:

> This imagery symbolizes deep racial hatred and discrimination that go against the core values of Bowie State University. The incident is being investigated as a possible hate crime by our campus police in collaboration with Prince George's County Police. We live in a community at Bowie State that values diversity, civility, vigorous debate and scholarly discussions. The imagery that was left seemed to be hateful and as such will not be tolerated. We do not tolerate hate speech among students, faculty or staff. We support those students who have decided to rally in opposition to hate speech.[88]

TeAna Brown, a senior at the school, told the school newspaper that "the quick response by university officials reassured students that they are safe at Bowie State."[89]

At the University of Michigan, messages in chalk appeared at the center of campus, reading "#StopIslam," "Trump 2016," and "Build the Wall," along with other messages. Nearly five hundred University of Michigan faculty members issued a statement denouncing the anti-Islam message on the school's campus. In an open letter they emphasized the "urgency of the situation" to develop a more inclusive campus.[90] "Whatever the political motivations of those engaged in such acts," the letter read, "their expressions of disrespect for members of our community can have nothing but a chilling effect on the social and intellectual life of this campus."[91] Campus officials also denounced the "repugnant" messages but noted students' right to speak.

On our campus, when conservative provocateur Milo Yiannopoulos was scheduled to appear and the administration faced demands to cancel the event, the vice chancellor for student affairs underscored our commitment to free speech and acknowledged that we must maintain a neutral position when faced with calls to silence certain voices. But he also noted that there was no requirement for neutrality when the university was deciding what values it would express. He continued: "We will not be neutral when acts of racism, bigotry, sexism, homophobia and oppression are paraded as sport intended to disrupt the cultural sensibilities of our diverse population. We will not be neutral when speakers and the crowds who support them use derogatory and vulgar language to insult and demean persons in our community on the basis of their race, citizenship status, gender or sexual orientation. We will not be neutral when degrading people's culture and history of struggle becomes comic relief for local and national audiences who seek to affirm themselves and their ideology by belittling others. That is not who we are as a university."[92]

"More speech" cannot undo the hurt caused by hateful speech. But a willingness of members of the campus community to speak out on behalf of the university's core values, and to condemn speech that is inimical to them, is an important component of how campuses should deal with offensive expression. Rather than be tempted toward censorship, campus leaders should focus on strategies premised on more speech.

At the same time, university officials cannot be expected to comment on or condemn every campus speech act that some person finds offensive. To encourage the widest diversity of views, colleges and universities should view themselves primarily as the home and sponsor of critics, not as institutions engaged in official editorializing on all expressed opinions.[93] The values articulated by campus officials should relate to the mission of colleges and universities and the importance of scholarly inquiry, teaching excellence, public service, and the free exchange of ideas. Frequent and persistent pronouncements by college or university leaders on the various views expressed within the community risk creating a campus orthodoxy of opinion, and it is the primary responsibility of campus officials to ensure that no such orthodoxy is established. Also, if campus officials speak out against every minor incident that offends someone, their comments are less likely to be effective when faced with more serious events. University officials are no more responsible for every view expressed on a campus than mayors are responsible for every view expressed by people in their cities, and their inability to issue condemnations of every controversial speech act cannot be interpreted as approval.

Still, there are times when views so assault the campus's basic values that leaders need to speak up. Obviously, this requires careful and inevitably controversial judgments about when and how campus leaders can most effectively exercise their free speech rights in a way that promotes the free exchange of ideas and fosters an inclusive learning community.

AN AGENDA FOR CAMPUSES

We have been very specific about what campuses can and can't do to reconcile free speech, academic freedom, and the need for an inclusive learning environment. Some people feel strongly that the last value requires compromising free expression, but we disagree. Still, our strong free speech views should not distract attention away from a wide range of activities that campuses can (and must) do to protect student well-being and promote an inclusive environment. For example, campuses can:

- Protect the rights of all students to engage in meaningful protest and to distribute materials that get their message out;
- Punish speech that constitutes "true threats" or that meets the definition of harassment under federal anti-discrimination law;
- Prevent disruptions of university activities;
- Ensure that campus dormitories are safe spaces of repose, short of imposing content-based restrictions on speech;
- Prevent discrimination by official campus organizations;

- Allow faculty to use trigger warnings when they deem it appropriate in light of their best pedagogical judgment;
- Sensitize the campus community to the harms caused by microaggressions and the effects of implicit bias;
- Ensure that learning environments are safe for the civil expression of ideas;
- Require institution-wide training on the obligation to create inclusive workplace and educational environments;
- Establish clear reporting requirements so that incidents of discriminatory practices can be quickly investigated and addressed;
- Establish clear and effective grievance procedures for those who believe the institution is not taking seriously its legal obligations to create nondiscriminatory workplace and learning environments;
- Prohibit retaliation against any person who complains about discriminatory workplace and learning environments;
- Promulgate clear and powerful principles of community, stressing the importance of an inclusive environment and condemning hateful or stigmatizing speech;
- Encourage faculty and students to research and learn about the harms associated with intolerance and structural discrimination, including through the creation of appropriate academic departments, the establishment of educational requirements

on diversity and structural inequality, the publication of research, and the sponsoring of academic symposia;

- Organize co-curricular activities that celebrate cultural diversity and provide victims of hateful and bullying acts the opportunity to be heard;
- Emphasize how the campus's scholarly mission is best accomplished when people of diverse backgrounds and perspectives work together in an environment of mutual respect and constructive engagement; and
- Speak out to condemn egregious acts of intolerance as a way of demonstrating the power of "more speech" rather than enforced silence.

CHAPTER SIX

What's at Stake?

SOME student activists and their supporters argue that an emphasis on free speech values is a "self-serving deflection" away from efforts to fight structural racism, everyday exclusion, and the marginalization of underrepresented students in higher education.[1] Jelani Cobb warns pro-speech advocates not to be "tone deaf" to these concerns, noting correctly that "the freedom to offend the powerful is not equivalent to the freedom to bully the relatively disempowered."[2] A Yale sophomore, reflecting on the controversies surrounding Erika Christakis's surprisingly explosive email about Halloween costumes, claimed that when a "false debate about 'free speech' is used to question people of color's humanity," that is "racism is disguise" and it "needs to stop."[3]

On many campuses, debates about free speech have put the problems of inclusion for historically excluded minorities, both in higher education and in the broader society, squarely on the table. There are many reasons for the continued underrepresentation at colleges and universities of African Americans, Hispanics, and Native Americans, especially those from disadvantaged backgrounds, and especially at more elite institutions.[4] It is the product of decades of systematic discrimination and implicit bias, racial segregation in housing, the underperformance of public schools in poor minority communities, state disinvestment in public higher education, legacy favoritism in private higher education, a lack of sufficient public support for affirmative action, and costs of attendance. On too many campuses, underrepresented minorities feel isolated and self-conscious in ways that should make us all understand the psychological harm they experience when they encounter hateful or even careless speech. Other populations of students—including first-generation college students, those from low-income families, religious minorities, and women entering male-dominated disciplines—experience similar challenges. These students have already proven themselves strong and capable of overcoming disadvantages, which is why it is wrong for commentators to characterize them as weak or pampered. Despite their accomplishments, every day they are on campus presents challenges, and exclusionary speech and microaggressions surely make things even harder.

Campuses must take these issues seriously. But the effort to create inclusive learning environments cannot proceed at the expense of free speech and academic freedom. Colleges and universities cannot accomplish their modern missions of knowledge creation and dissemination unless their scholars and students are free to think and express any idea, especially those that challenge or test conventional wisdom. But colleges and universities also cannot accomplish their modern missions if they are places of privilege and exclusion rather than gateways of inclusive excellence.

We wrote this book out of a concern that much of the current debate over the learning environment on college campuses gives insufficient attention to the values of free speech and academic freedom—the philosophical, moral, and practical arguments in support of these principles, the lessons of the historical record, and the current state of the law. Surveys reveal that students' support for basic free speech principles is dramatically eroding.[5] It has to be explained over and over that the First Amendment contains no exception for hate speech.[6] There are too many efforts to censor or punish clearly protected political speech and to deny controversial speakers the right to address campus communities. The differences between the protection and regulation of academic freedom and the protection of free speech in the public square are not always well understood even by faculty members and administrators. College and university leaders are well versed in providing full-throated defenses of civility and tolerance, but their arguments for protecting the expression of all ideas, even those considered offensive and hateful, are often less clear or convincing. The Department of Education's Office of Civil Rights, which is dedicated to opposing discrimination in higher education, has created an environment whereby formal investigations can be triggered by clearly protected speech, and it is giving guidance to colleges and universities that conflicts with the First Amendment.

As a first step toward improving the quality of the conversation, it is vital for campuses to more clearly identify liberty of thought, unfettered inquiry, and robust debate as foundational values within higher education, pro-actively educate their communities on these values, and recommit to their protection in the face of calls to subordinate these values to other ideals. Campus leaders should underscore the importance of providing a forum for unpopular and controversial views, and should be prepared to treat disruptive protests as violations of both free speech and campus codes of conduct.

We are not the first to face the challenge of re-defending these rights. In the early 1970s Yale University experienced a number of episodes involving efforts to silence or disrupt certain controversial speakers.[7] The most heated debates involved William Shockley, a famed Stanford University physicist and inventor, who later in life became infamous for expressing the view that "the major cause of the American Negros' intellectual and social deficits is hereditary and racially genetic in origin and, thus, not remediable to a major degree by practical improvements in the environment." Among other measures, Shockley advocated voluntary sterilization within the African American community.[8]

Shockley had been invited to debate Roy I. Innis, executive director of the Congress of Racial Equality, about these views, and the campus endured months of heated debate over whether to rescind the invitation.[9] After Shockley's scheduled appearance was disrupted by protests, the Yale College faculty requested that President Kingman Brewster Jr. "appoint a faculty commission to examine the condition of free expression, peaceful dissent, mutual respect and tolerance at Yale" and to "draft recommendations for any measures it may deem necessary for the maintenance of those principles." The result was the Woodward Report, named after its chair, the distinguished historian C. Vann Woodward. The report reiterated that "the university must do everything possible to ensure within it the fullest degree of intellectual freedom," including "the right to think the unthinkable, discuss the unmentionable, and challenge the unchallengeable." On the question of how to balance the free exchange of ideas against the need to create a supportive community, the committee wrote:

> If a university is a place for knowledge, it is also a special kind of small society, . . . not primarily a fellowship, a club, a circle of friends, a replica of civil society outside it. Without sacrificing its central purpose, it cannot make its primary and dominant value the fostering of friendship, solidarity, harmony, civility, or mutual respect. To be sure, these are important values; other institutions may properly assign them the highest, and not merely a subordinate priority; and a good university will seek and may in some significant measure attain these ends. But it will never let these values, important as they are, override its central purpose. We value freedom of expression precisely because it provides a forum for the new, the provocative, the disturbing, and the unorthodox. Free speech is a barrier to the tyranny of authoritarian or even majority opinion as to the rightness or wrongness of particular doctrines or thoughts.[10]

Among the committee's key recommendations was that the university develop "a program of reeducation" to help members of the community "appreciate the value of the principle of freedom of expression." This program would include helping protestors "understand the limits of protest in a community committed to the principles of free speech," with special attention to the principle that there is no right to disrupt a university activity.

A renewed appreciation of the value of free expression is important, not only for life on contemporary college campuses but also for the future of civic discourse and democratic practice in the United States. The worrisome tendencies at colleges and universities to punish or silence the expression of ideas occur amid similar tendencies in the broader political system. Deep, persistent ideological divisions in society are leading many to treat political opponents as enemies, shout down critics, and reject compromise. With the collapse of traditional network news and the rise of "curated" information-gathering on cable and online, it is easier for people to listen only to those with whom they already agree, and to respond to opposing viewpoints with mockery and suspicion of ill intent.

These are troubling developments. It is not possible for a diverse, democratic society to survive without some measure of tolerance for opposing viewpoints, respect for people who hold different views, and a willingness to discuss and debate across lines of difference—a bundle of norms and practices that amounts to "hearing the other side."[11] American colleges and universities should be a corrective. They should stand as models for how diverse communities of people work together to address important and difficult questions. Campuses make their strongest contributions to free societies when a lively and diverse campus community shows a genuine desire to engage competing perspectives, learn from those who have had different experiences or hold different viewpoints, engage and rebut ideas considered harmful or dangerous, and resolve disagreements through rational argumentation, evidence-based reasoning, and the acquisition of new knowledge.

Promoting an inclusive culture of mutual respect, tolerating diverse and controversial views, and working through differences by way of conversation rather than intimidation are essential not only to higher education. They are also how free, diverse, democratic societies must behave if they are to remain free, diverse, and democratic.

The generation now in college will soon be our society's leaders. The stakes could not be higher as we help them understand why free speech matters, not just on campuses but in the world. If we expect them to fight for these values, we must teach them these values.

Notes

CHAPTER I. THE NEW CENSORSHIP

1. Steve Szkotak, *"Muzzles" Mine Rich Vein of Speech Limits Among U.S. Colleges,* ASSOCIATED PRESS (Apr. 20, 2016), http://www.bigstory. ap.org/article/2187e1e72eef46ce8486b25039066750/muzzles-mine-rich-vein-speech-limits-among-us-colleges.

2. *See U. of Tulsa Suspends Student for Someone Else's Facebook Post,* FOUND. FOR INDIVIDUAL RIGHTS IN EDUC. (Feb. 12, 2015), https://www.thefire.org/u-tulsa-suspends-student-someone-elses-facebook-post/.

3. *See* Laura Kipnis, *Sexual Paranoia Strikes Academe,* CHRON. HIGHER EDUC. (Feb. 27, 2015), http://chronicle.com/article/Sexual-Paranoia-Strikes/190351/.

4. *Id.*

5. Laura Kipnis, *My Title IX Inquisition,* CHRON. HIGHER EDUC. (May 29, 2015), http://chronicle.com/article/My-Title-IX-Inquisition/230489/.

6. *See* Eugene Volokh, *No, It's Not Constitutional for the University of Oklahoma to Expel Students For Racist Speech [Updated in Light of the Students' Expulsion],* WASH. POST: VOLOKH CONSPIRACY (Mar. 10, 2015), https://www.washingtonpost.com/news/volokh-conspiracy/wp/2015/03/10/no-a-public-university-may-not-expel-students-for-racist-speech/.

7. Eugene Volokh, *Youngstown State University Student Government Removes "Straight Pride" Posters [Updated]*, WASH. POST: VOLOKH CONSPIRACY (Apr. 24, 2015), https://www.washingtonpost.com/news/volokh-conspiracy/wp/2015/04/24/youngstown-state-university-student-government-removes-straight-pride-posters/.

8. *See Texas Christian University Tramples Student's Rights in Order to Appease Angry Internet Mob*, FOUND. FOR INDIVIDUAL RIGHTS IN EDUC. (July 29, 2015), https://www.thefire.org/texas-christian-university-tramples-students-rights/.

9. *See Findings and Sanction Letter from TCU*, FOUND. FOR INDIVIDUAL RIGHTS IN EDUC. (July 28, 2015), https://www.thefire.org/findings-and-sanction-letter-from-tcu/.

10. *Letter Upholding Findings and Sanctions*, FOUND. FOR INDIVIDUAL RIGHTS IN EDUC. (July 28, 2015), https://www.thefire.org/letter-upholding-findings-and-sanctions/.

11. *See* Eugene Volokh, *UCLA Likely Violating First Amendment in Its Reaction to Kim-Kardashian/Kanye-West-Themed Fraternity/Sorority Party*, WASH. POST: VOLOKH CONSPIRACY (Oct. 12, 2015), https://www.washingtonpost.com/news/volokh-conspiracy/wp/2015/10/12/ucla-likely-violating-first-amendment-in-its-reaction-to-kim-kardashiankanye-west-themed-fraternitysorority-party/.

12. Editorial Board, *Editorial: Greek Life Needs Policing to Prevent More "Kanye Western" Type Raids*, DAILY BRUIN (Oct. 12, 2015, 1:53 am), http://dailybruin.com/2015/10/12/editorial-greek-life-needs-policing-to-prevent-more-kanye-western-type-raids/.

13. *Email from the Intercultural Affairs Committee*, FOUND. FOR INDIVIDUAL RIGHTS IN EDUC. (Oct. 27, 2015), https://www.thefire.org/email-from-intercultural-affairs/.

14. *Email from Erika Christakis: "Dressing Yourselves," Email to Silliman College (Yale) Students on Halloween Costumes*, FOUND. FOR INDIVIDUAL RIGHTS IN EDUC. (Oct. 30, 2015), https://www.thefire.org/email-from-erika-christakis-dressing-yourselves-email-to-silliman-college-yale-students-on-halloween-costumes/.

15. *See* Greg Lukianoff, *On the Front Lines of the Fight for Free Speech at Yale*, WASH. POST: GRADE POINT (Nov. 11, 2015), https://www.washingtonpost.com/news/grade-point/wp/2015/11/11/on-the-front-lines-of-the-fight-for-free-speech-at-yale/.

16. *Open Letter to Associate Master Christakis*, Down Mag (Oct. 31, 2015), http://downatyale.com/post.php?id=430.

17. *See* Isaac Stanley-Becker, *Yale Instructor at the Center of Racial Protest to Leave Teaching Role*, Wash. Post: Grade Point (Dec. 4, 2015), https://www.washingtonpost.com/news/grade-point/wp/2015/12/04/with-her-words-this-instructor-helped-set-off-protests-over-race-and-a-debate-over-free-speech-now-shes-leaving-yale/. A year later, Erika Christakis wrote an op-ed in the *Washington Post* decrying the culture of censorship that forced her out of Yale after this incident. Erika Christakis, *My Halloween Email Led to a Campus Firestorm—And a Troubling Lesson About Self Censorship*, Wash. Post (Oct. 28, 2016), https://www.washingtonpost.com/opinions/my-halloween-email-led-to-a-campus-firestorm--and-a-troubling-lesson-about-self-censorship/2016/10/28/70e55732–9b97–11e6-a0ed-ab0774c1eaa5_story.html.

18. *Colorado College Suspends Student for Two Years for Six-Word Joke on Yik Yak*, Found. for Individual Rights in Educ. (Dec. 7, 2015), https://www.thefire.org/colorado-college-suspends-student-for-two-years-for-six-word-joke-on-yik-yak/.

19. *See id.*

20. *See* Katie Rogers, *Pro-Trump Chalk Messages Cause Conflicts on College Campuses*, N.Y. Times (Apr. 1, 2016), http://www.nytimes.com/2016/04/02/us/pro-trump-chalk-messages-cause-conflicts-on-college-campuses.html.

21. Chris Marchese, *"The Chalkening" Spreads, Tests Universities' Commitment to Free* Speech, Found. for Individual Rights in Educ. (Apr. 13, 2016), https://www.thefire.org/the-chalkening-spreads-tests-universities-commitment-to-free-speech/.

22. Richard Pérez-Peña et al., *University of Chicago Strikes Back Against Campus Political Correctness*, N.Y. Times (Aug. 26, 2016).

23. Valerie Strauss, *So You Like the University of Chicago's Rejection of Safe Spaces for Students, Consider This*, Wash. Post (Aug. 30, 2016), https://www.washingtonpost.com/news/answer-sheet/wp/2016/08/30/so-you-like-the-university-of-chicagos-rejection-of-safe-spaces-for-students-consider-this/?utm_term=.636a53767f36.

24. Cameron Luttrell, *University of Chicago Staff Members Critique Dean's Controversial Letter*, http://patch.com/illinois/hydepark/

university-chicago-staff-members-critique-deans-controversial-letter (Sept. 14, 2016).

25. *"Stupid and Offensive,"* UO MATTERS (Nov. 2, 2016), http://uomatters.com/2016/11/stupid-and-offensive.html.

26. *Id.* and *University of Oregon Investigative Report* (Nov. 20, 2016), https://provost.uoregon.edu/sites/provost.uoregon.edu/files/final_investigative_report_redacted_-_final.pdf.

27. A report by PEN America, released in October 2016, came to the same conclusion: "Recent incidents have raised significant concerns about the heated climate for intellectual life on U.S. campuses and the implications for the rising generation of college-educated Americans." *And Campus for All: Diversity, Inclusion, and Freedom of Speech at U.S. Universities,* https://pen.org/sites/default/files/PEN_campus_report_final_online_2.pdf.

28. *Survey: Half of U.S. College Students "Intimidated" When Sharing Views,* WILLIAM F. BUCKLEY, JR. PROGRAM AT YALE (Oct. 26, 2015), http://www.buckleyprogram.com/#!SURVEY-Half-of-US-College-Students-Intimidated-When-Sharing-Views/c18lp/igaxoon420.

29. For the contrary view by a First Amendment professor that the expulsion was unconstitutional, see Eugene Volokh, *No, It's Not Constitutional for the University of Oklahoma to Expel Students For Racist Speech [Updated in Light of the Students' Expulsion],* WASH. POST: VOLOKH CONSPIRACY (Mar. 10, 2015), https://www.washingtonpost.com/news/volokh-conspiracy/wp/2015/03/10/no-a-public-university-may-not-expel-students-for-racist-speech/.

30. *See* Jacob Poushter, *40% of Millennials OK with Limiting Speech Offensive to Minorities,* PEW RESEARCH CTR. (Nov. 20, 2015), http://www.pewresearch.org/fact-tank/2015/11/20/40-of-millennials-ok-with-limiting-speech-offensive-to-minorities/.

31. *See* Jo Freeman, *The Berkeley Free Speech Movement, in* ENCYC. OF AM. SOC. MOVEMENTS, 1178–82 (Immanuel Ness, ed., 2004).

32. *See* David R. Wheeler, *Do Students Still Have Free Speech in School?* ATLANTIC (Apr. 7, 2014), http://www.theatlantic.com/education/archive/2014/04/do-students-still-have-free-speech-in-school/360266/.

33. *See* Tasnim Shamma, *Yik Yak Tests Universities' Defense of Free Speech,* NPR (Jan. 23, 2016, 5:12 pm), http://www.npr.org/sections/

alltechconsidered/2016/01/23/463197593/yik-yak-tests-universities-defense-of-free-speech.

34. *See* Nat'l Coalition Against Censorship, NCAC to Dept. of Ed: Vague Definition of Harassment Threatens Student Free Speech, http://ncac.org/resource/are-department-of-education-policies-hurting-campus-free-speech (last visited July 20, 2016).

35. *U. of California at Irvine Cleared in Investigation of Anti-Semitism,* Chron. Higher Educ. (Dec. 12, 2007), http://chronicle.com/article/U-of-California-at-Irvine/40124.

36. *Two More UC Campuses Cleared in U.S. Probes of Anti-Semitism,* L.A. Times (Aug. 28, 2013), http://articles.latimes.com/2013/aug/28/local/la-me-ln-uc-jewish–20130828.

37. *See OCR's Investigation of U. of Mary Washington Raises Free Speech Concerns,* Found. for Individual Rights in Educ. (Oct. 22, 2015), https://www.thefire.org/ocrs-investigation-of-u-of-mary-washington-raises-free-speech-concerns/.

38. Gerald A. Reynolds, *First Amendment: Dear Colleague,* U.S. Dep't of Educ. (July 28, 2003), http://www2.ed.gov/about/offices/list/ocr/firstamend.html.

39. *Id.*

40. *See* Susan Kruth, *DOJ Demands Clarity from UNM While Mandating Confusing Sexual Harassment Policy,* Found. for Individual Rights in Educ. (Apr. 27, 2016), https://www.thefire.org/doj-demands-clarity-from-unm-while-mandating-confusing-sexual-harassment-policy/.

41. *See* U.S. Dep't of Educ., Revised Sexual Harassment Guidance: Harassment of Students By School Employees, Other Students, or Third Parties Title IX (Jan. 19, 2001), http://www2.ed.gov/about/offices/list/ocr/docs/shguide.html. We discuss the issue of harassment in detail in Chapter 5.

42. Greg Lukianoff and Jonathan Haidt, *The Coddling of the American Mind,* Atlantic at 42–52 (Sept. 2015). Lukianoff also develops this theme in his book, Unlearning Liberty: Campus Censorship and the End of American Debate (2014).

43. Lukianoff and Haidt, *The Coddling of the American Mind.*

CHAPTER 2. WHY IS FREE SPEECH IMPORTANT?

1. *Palko v. Connecticut*, 302 U.S. 319, 327 (1937).

2. *Thomas v. Collins*, 323 U.S. 516, 529 (1945).

3. See Steven Pinker, *Why Free Speech Is Fundamental*, BOSTON GLOBE (Jan. 27, 2015), https://www.bostonglobe.com/opinion/2015/01/26/why-free-speech-fundamental/aaAWVYFscrhFCC4ye9FVjN/story.html, and Thomas L. Emerson, THE SYSTEM OF FREEDOM OF EXPRESSION (1970), for elaboration on some of these points and additional thoughts.

4. *See* George Orwell, 1984: A NOVEL (1949).

5. *U.S. v. Schwimmer*, 279 U.S. 644, 654–55 (1929).

6. Benjamin Franklin, *On Freedom of Speech and the Press*, PENNSYLVANIA GAZETTE (Nov. 17, 1737).

7. Letter from Thomas Jefferson to Edward Carrington (Jan. 16, 1787), *in* 11 THE PAPERS OF THOMAS JEFFERSON, at 48–49 (Julian P. Boyd et al., eds., 1950).

8. *See* Pinker, *Why Free Speech Is Fundamental*.

9. Robert Justin Goldstein, POLITICAL CENSORSHIP OF THE ARTS AND THE PRESS IN NINETEENTH-CENTURY EUROPE 34 (1989).

10. Mark A. Graber and Howard Gillman, 1 THE COMPLETE AMERICAN CONSTITUTIONALISM: INTRODUCTION AND THE CO-LONIAL ERA, at 356–61 (2015).

11. *See* John Milton, AREOPAGITICA (1961) (1738).

12. *Id.* at 51.

13. *Id.* at 149.

14. John Marshall, JOHN LOCKE, TOLERATION AND EARLY EN-LIGHTENMENT CULTURE 680 (2006). Because the idea of toleration was at an early stage of development, it should come as no surprise that there were limits to Locke's version of it. The Roman Catholic Church could not be tolerated in England, he thought, because "all those who enter into it do thereby ipso facto deliver themselves up to the protection and service of another prince." *Id.* at 690. There is controversy among scholars whether Locke was willing to tolerate atheists.

15. John Trenchard and Thomas Gordon, 1 CATO'S LETTERS, at 98 (1723).

16. 5 William Blackstone, COMMENTARIES *151–52.

17. MERRIAM-WEBSTER'S COLLEGIATE DICTIONARY (11th ed. 2008).

18. *See* James P. Martin, *When Repression Is Democratic and Constitutional: The Federalist Theory of Representation and the Sedition Act of 1798*, 66 U. Chi. L. Rev. 117 (1999).

19. *See, e.g., State v. Worth*, 52 N.C. 488 (1860).

20. Richard R. John, *Highland Hall's "Report on Incendiary Publications": A Forgotten Nineteenth Century Defense of the Constitutional Guarantee of the Freedom of the Press*, *in* 41 American Journal of Legal History, at 94 (1997).

21. Janice Ruth Wood, The Struggle for Free Speech in the United States, 1872–1915: Edward Bliss Foote, Edward Bond Foote, and Anti-Comstock Operations 41 (2011).

22. *See* Mark A. Graber, Transforming Free Speech: The Ambiguous Legacy of Civil Libertarianism (1992).

23. Woodrow Wilson, *Third Annual Message* (Dec. 7, 1915), *available at* American Presidency Project, http://www.presidency.ucsb.edu/ws/?pid=29556.

24. *See* Geoffrey R. Stone, Perilous Times: Free Speech in Wartime from the Sedition Act of 1798 to the War on Terror (2005).

25. 249 U.S. 47 (1919).

26. *Id.* at 52.

27. *See Debs v. U.S.*, 249 U.S. 211 (1919). While sitting in prison, Debs ran for president. He received almost a million votes, or 3.4 percent of the popular vote.

28. *See* Christopher Finan, From the Palmer Raids to the Patriot Act: A History of the Fight for Free Speech in America (2008).

29. *See* Nat'l Popular Government League, To the American People: Report Upon the Illegal Practices of the United States Department of Justice (1920).

30. *See* Zachariah Chaffee, Freedom of Speech (1920).

31. For an explanation of how Holmes came to change his mind about speech protections since his *Debs* opinion, see Thomas Healy, The Great Dissent: How Oliver Wendell Holmes Changed His Mind — and Changed the History of Free Speech in America (2013).

32. *Abrams v. U.S.*, 250 U.S. 616 (1919).

33. *Id.* at 630.

34. 274 U.S. 357 (1927).

35. *Id.* at 371.

36. *Id.* at 376.

37. *Id.* at 377.

38. *DeJonge v. Oregon,* 299 U.S. 353 (1937); *Herndon v. Lowry,* 301 U.S. 242 (1937).

39. *Palko,* 302 U.S. at 327.

40. 319 U.S. 624, 642 (1943).

41. 325 U.S. 478 (1945).

42. *Thomas v. Collins,* 323 U.S. 516, 530 (1945).

43. *See* Stone, PERILOUS TIMES.

44. *Dennis v. U.S.,* 341 U.S. 494 (1951).

45. *Id.* at 511–12.

46. 354 U.S. 298, 318 (1957).

47. *Id.* at 343–44.

48. Taylor Branch, PARTING THE WATERS: AMERICA IN THE KING YEARS, 1954–63, at 181–82, 468–69 (1988).

49. *NAACP v. Alabama,* 357 U.S. 449 (1958).

50. *NAACP v. Button,* 371 U.S. 415 (1963).

51. *Garner v. Louisiana,* 368 U.S. 157 (1961).

52. *N.Y. Times v. Sullivan,* 376 U.S. 254 (1964).

53. *Bell v. Maryland,* 378 U.S. 226 (1964).

54. *U.S. v. O'Brien,* 391 U.S. 367 (1968).

55. 395 U.S. 444, 446 (1969).

56. *Id.* at 447.

57. *Brandenburg,* 395 U.S. at 449.

58. 403 U.S. 15 (1971).

59. *Id.* at 23.

60. *Id.* at 25.

61. *Id.*

62. 343 U.S. 495, 505 (1952).

63. *Cohen v. Cal.,* 403 U.S. 15, 25 (1971).

64. In *Alexander v. U.S.,* 509 U.S. 544 (1993), a closely divided Supreme Court upheld applying racketeering (RICO) laws to destroy $9 million of merchandise owned by a man who was sentenced to six years in prison for selling seven obscene items.

65. *Abrams*, 250 U.S. at 630.

CHAPTER 3. *NULLIUS IN VERBA*

1. *See* 1 A History of the University in Europe: Universities in the Middle Ages, at 47–55 (Hilde de Ridder-Symoens, ed.) (1992).

2. Gregory W. Dawes, Galileo and the Conflict Between Religion and Science 68 (2016). The Church's position was more nuanced than is commonly believed; *see* Ronald L. Numbers, Galileo Goes to Jail and Other Myths about Science and Religion 68–78 (2010)

3. Maurice A. Finocchiaro, The Galileo Affair: A Documentary History 147 (1989).

4. *See* Freeman J. Dyson, Dreams of Earth and Sky (2015); *see also* the history of the Royal Society as summarized on the official website, The Royal Society, History, *available at* https://royalsociety.org/about-us/history/. At the time it would have been recognized as an abbreviated version of a well-known line of the poet Horace: "Sworn to follow the words of no master."

5. Isaac Newton, Philosophiae Naturalis Principia Mathematica (Project Gutenberg Literary Archive Found., 2009) (1687).

6. The Royal Society, History, *available at* https://royalsociety.org/about-us/history/.

7. *See* Yale U. Libr., Resources on Yale History: A Brief History of Yale, *available at* http://guides.library.yale.edu/yalehistory.

8. *See* Dartmouth Rauner Libr., Dartmouth History: A Dartmouth History Lesson for Freshmen, *available at* http://www.dartmouth.edu/~library/rauner/dartmouth/dartmouth_history.html?mswitch-redir=classic.

9. *See* Stephen J. Nelson, The Shape and Shaping of the College and University in America 186 (2016).

10. Walter P. Metzger, Academic Freedom in the Age of the University 4–5 (1961).

11. 1 American Higher Education: A Documentary History 258 (Richard Hofstadter and Wilson Smith, eds., 1961).

12. Metzger, ACADEMIC FREEDOM IN THE AGE OF THE UNIVERSITY, at 100.

13. *From Thomas Jefferson to William Roscoe* (Dec. 27, 1820), Nat'l Archives Founders Online, http://founders.archives.gov/documents/Jefferson/98–01–02–1712.

14. Charles Lyell, PRINCIPLES OF GEOLOGY (1991) (1830–33).

15. Charles Darwin, THE ORIGIN OF SPECIES (1996) (1859).

16. *See* AMERICAN HIGHER EDUCATION, at 56.

17. *Id.* at 65.

18. *See* Clark Kerr, THE GREAT TRANSFORMATION IN HIGHER EDUCATION, 1960–1980, 218 (1991); *see also* Jonathan R. Cole, THE GREAT AMERICAN UNIVERSITY: ITS RISE TO PREEMINENCE, ITS INDISPENSABLE NATIONAL ROLE, WHY IT MUST BE PROTECTED 16–22 (2009).

19. George M. Marsden, THE SOUL OF THE AMERICAN UNIVERSITY: FROM PROTESTANT ESTABLISHMENT TO ESTABLISHED NONBELIEF 113–14, 116 (1994).

20. *See id.* at 142.

21. *Id.* at 151.

22. Nelson, THE SHAPE AND SHAPING OF THE COLLEGE AND UNIVERSITY IN AMERICA, at 196. The phrase "sifting and winnowing" was secretly authored by the university's president Charles Adams.

23. *See id.* at 196–99. Jane Stanford also expressed frustration with Ross's views on Asian immigration, which were racist and xenophobic. *See* Brian Eule, *Watch Your Words, Professor,* STANFORD (Jan./Feb. 2015), https://alumni.stanford.edu/get/page/magazine/article/?article_id=75857.

24. Nelson, THE SHAPE AND SHAPING OF THE COLLEGE AND UNIVERSITY IN AMERICA, at 199.

25. John W. Boyer, THE UNIVERSITY OF CHICAGO: A HISTORY 263 (2015).

26. Geoffrey R. Stone, PERILOUS TIMES: FREE SPEECH IN WARTIME FROM THE SEDITION ACT OF 1798 TO THE WAR ON TERRORISM 317 (2004).

27. *See* American Association of University Professors, HISTORY OF THE AAUP, *available at* https://www.aaup.org/about/history-aaup.

28. Metzger, THE SHAPE AND SHAPING OF THE COLLEGE AND UNIVERSITY IN AMERICA, at 205.

29. *See* HISTORY OF THE AAUP.

30. John Dewey, *The Social Significance of Academic Freedom, in* THE LATER WORKS OF JOHN DEWEY, 1925–1953, at 378 (Jo Ann Boydston, ed., 1987) (1936).

31. FREEDOM AND TENURE IN THE ACADEMY 401 (William W. Van Alstyne, ed., 1993) (1915).

32. 34 AMERICAN EDUCATIONAL HISTORY JOURNAL 290 (J. Wesley Null et al., eds. 2007).

33. Ellen Schrecker, *Academic Freedom and the Cold War,* 38 ANTIOCH REVIEW 313–27, 317–18 (1980).

34. *See id.* at 319–27 and AAUP, *Academic Freedom and Tenure in the Quest for National Security,* 42 AAUP BULL. 49, 57–58 (1956).

35. *Slochower v. Bd. of Higher Educ.,* 350 U.S. 551, 564 n.6 (1956).

36. Richard Ohmann, *Academic Freedom's Best Days,* INSIDE HIGHER ED. (Apr. 19, 2011), https://www.insidehighered.com/views/2011/04/19/academic-freedoms-best-days.

37. *See* Richard J. Herrnstein and Charles Murray, THE BELL CURVE: INTELLIGENCE AND CLASS STRUCTURE IN AMERICAN LIFE (1994).

38. *See* Nicholas Lemann, *The Bell Curve Flattened: Subsequent Research Has Seriously Undercut the Claims of the Controversial Best Seller,* SLATE, Jan. 18, 1997, *available at* http://www.slate.com/articles/briefing/articles/1997/01/the_bell_curve_flattened.html.

39. *See id.*

40. The APA's formal response was published in a 1996 report. *See* Ulric Nessier et al., *Intelligence: Knowns and Unknowns,* 51 AM. PSYCH. 77 (1996).

41. *See* William J. Matthews, *A Review of the Bell Curve: Bad Science Makes for Bad Conclusions* (1994), https://bolesblogs.com/1998/03/23/a-review-of-the-bell-curve-bad-science-makes-for-bad-conclusions/; *see also* Stephen Jay Gould, THE MISMEASURE OF MAN (1996).

42. Examples of scholarly and other academic critiques of the work are extensive, but for a start, see Steven Fraser, BELL CURVE WARS: RACE, INTELLIGENCE, AND THE FUTURE OF AMERICA (1995).

43. American Association of University Professors, *Ensuring Academic Freedom in Politically Controversial Academic Personnel Decisions*, https://www.aaup.org/report/ensuring-academic-freedom-politically-controversial-academic-personnel-decisions.

44. *Id.*

45. 11 American Association of University Professors, *Policy Documents and Reports*, at 11 (2015).

46. Cass R. Sunstein, *Academic Freedom and Law: Liberalism, Speech Codes, and Related Problems, in* THE FUTURE OF ACADEMIC FREEDOM, 107 (Louis Menand, ed., 1996).

47. U. of Cal., Academic Policy Manual: Academic Freedom (2003), *available at* http://www.ucop.edu/academic-personnel-programs/_files/apm/apm–010.pdf.

48. *See id.*

49. *Id.*

50. *See Waters v. Churchill*, 511 U.S. 661 (1994). One controversial example involved CUNY Professor Leonard Jeffries, who while chair of the Black Studies Department advocated the view that Jews financed the slave trade and used the movie industry to hurt black people. There was a lengthy legal battle after he was discharged from his administrative leadership position (while being allowed to continue as a faculty member), and after back-and-forth decisions, a federal appeals court upheld his removal. *See Jeffries v. Harleston*, 52 F.3d 9 (1995). When Oberlin College dismissed a faculty member after she claimed on social media that "Israeli and Zionist Jews" were responsible for the 9/11 and *Charlie Hebdo* terrorist attacks, the board of trustees emphasized that the finding, made after a recommendation of the executive body of Oberlin's faculty, focused on her "professional integrity and fitness" as defined by the AAUP's "Statement of Professional Ethics," which requires that faculty members "accept the obligation to exercise critical self-discipline and judgment in using, extending and transmitting knowledge" and to "practice intellectual honesty." See Andrew Mytelka, *Oberlin College Fires Professor over Anti-Semitic Media Posts*, CHRON. OF HIGHER ED. (Nov. 16, 2016), http://www.chronicle.com/blogs/ticker/oberlin-college-fires-professor-over-anti-semitic-social-media-posts/115587, and Oberlin News Center, *Board of Trustees Statement on Assistant Professor Joy Karega* (Nov. 17, 2016), http://news.oberlin.edu/articles/board-trustees-statement-assistant-professor-joy-karega/.

51. See Scott E. Page, THE DIFFERENCE: HOW THE POWER OF DIVERSITY CREATES BETTER GROUPS, FIRMS, SCHOOLS, AND SOCIETIES (2007), and Jose L. Duarte et al., *Political Diversity Will Improve Social Psychological Science*, BEHAVIORAL AND BRAIN SCIENCES, Vol. 38 (Jan. 2015), https://www.cambridge.org/core/journals/behavioral-and-brain-sciences/article/political-diversity-will-improve-social-psychological-science–1/A54AD4878AED1AFC8BA6AF54A890149F.

52. Albert Einstein, OUT OF MY LATER YEARS 13 (1940).

53. See Beth McMurtie, *One University Asks: How Do You Promote Free Speech Without Alienating Students*, CHRON. OF HIGHER ED. (Oct. 23, 2016), http://www.chronicle.com/article/One-University-Asks-How-Do/238146 and Rachel Hinton, *University Denies Second Yiannopoulos Visit*, THE DEPAULIA (July 7, 2016), http://depauliaonline.com/2016/07/07/university-denies-second-yiannopoulus-visit/.

54. *See* Josh Logue, *Another Speaker Blocked*, INSIDE HIGHER ED. (Feb. 24, 2016), https://www.insidehighered.com/news/2016/02/24/cal-state-los-angeles-cancels-conservative-speakers-appearance and Kristine Guerre, *Protests Derail UD Davis Event with Breitbart's Milo Yiannopoulos, "Pharma Bro" Martin Shkreli*, WASH. POST (Jan. 14, 2017), https://www.washingtonpost.com/news/grade-point/wp/2017/01/14/protests-derail-uc-davis-event-with-breitbarts-milo-yiannopoulos-pharma-bro-martin-shkreli/?utm_term=.445c5a3f7ea9.

55. *See* Catherine Rampell, *Free Speech Is Flunking Out on College Campuses*, WASH. POST (Oct. 22, 2015), https://www.washingtonpost.com/opinions/free-speech-is-flunking-out-on-college-campuses/2015/10/22/124e7cd2–78f5–11e5–b9c1–f03c48c96ac2_story.html; *see also* Kate Talerico, *When Student Activists Refuse to Talk to Campus Newspapers*, ATLANTIC (June 30, 2016), http://www.theatlantic.com/education/archive/2016/06/when-student-activists-refuse-to-talk-to-campus-newspapers/486326/.

56. *See* Kim D. Chanbonpin, *Crisis and Trigger Warnings: Reflections on Legal Education and the Social Value of the Law*, 90 CHI.-KENT L. REV. 615 (2015).

57. *See* Teresa Watanabe and Carla Rivera, *Amid Racial Bias Protests, Claremont McKenna Dean Resigns*, L.A. TIMES (Nov. 13, 2015), http://www.latimes.com/local/lanow/la-me-ln-claremont-marches–20151112-story.html; *see also* Conor Friedersdorf, *The Perils of Writing a Provocative*

Email at Yale, ATLANTIC (May 26, 2016), http://www.theatlantic.com/politics/archive/2016/05/the-peril-of-writing-a-provocative-email-at-yale/484418/, and Erika Christakis, *My Halloween Email Led to a Campus Firestorm—and a Troubling Lesson About Self-Censorship*, WASH. POST (Oct. 28, 2016), https://www.washingtonpost.com/opinions/my-halloween-email-led-to-a-campus-firestorm--and-a-troubling-lesson-about-self-censorship/2016/10/28/70e55732–9b97–11e6-a0ed-ab-0774c1eaa5_story.html.

58. For more information on the UK NUS, see UK Nat'l Union of Students, *Who We Are*, *available at* http://www.nus.org.uk/en/who-we-are/, and Evan Smith, *A Policy Widely Abused: The Origins of the "No Platform" Policy of the National Union of Students*, HISTORY AND POLICY (March 23, 2016), http://www.historyandpolicy.org/opinion-articles/articles/a-policy-widely-abused.

59. *See* Sarah Bell, *NUS "Right to Have No Platform Policy,"* BBC NEWS (Apr. 25, 2016), http://www.bbc.com/news/education–36101423.

60. *See* Rachael Pells, *NUS "No Platform" Policy Goes "Too Far" and Threatens Free Speech, Peter Tatchell Warns*, THE INDEP. (April 25, 2016), http://www.independent.co.uk/news/uk/nus-no-platform-safe-space-policy-goes-too-far-threatens-free-speech-warns-peter-tatchell-a6999801.html; *see also* Sarah Ditum, *"No Platform" Was Once Reserved for Violent Fascists. Now It's Being Used to Silence Debate*, NEW STATESMAN (March 18, 2014), http://www.newstatesman.com/sarah-ditum/2014/03/when-did-no-platform-become-about-attacking-individuals-deemed-disagreeable.

61. *See* Pells, *NUS "No Platform" Policy Goes "Too Far."*

62. *See* Sarah Brown and Katherine Mangan, *What "Safe Spaces" Really Look Like on College Campuses*, CHRON. OF HIGHER ED. (Sept. 8, 2016), http://www.chronicle.com/article/What-Safe-Spaces-Really/237720, and Emily Crockett, *Safe Spaces, Explained*, VOX (Aug. 25, 2016), http://www.vox.com/2016/7/5/11949258/safe-spaces-explained.

63. We discuss the concept of safe spaces in more detail in Chapter 5.

64. *See* Debbi Baker, *UCSD Students Call Trump Messages Chalked on Campus Racist*, SAN DIEGO TRIB. (April 12, 2016), http://www.sandiegouniontribune.com/news/2016/apr/12/ucsd-students-offended-trump-messages-on-campus/.

65. *See Conservative Christian Organization Sues Cal State LA President Over Speech Spat*, L.A. DAILY NEWS (May 19, 2016), http://www.dailynews.com/general-news/20160519/conservative-christian-organization-sues-cal-state-la-president-over-speech-spat.

66. *See* Jessica Chasmar, *University of Houston Defends Free Speech After Student's "All Lives Matter" Post*, WASH. TIMES (July 15, 2016), http://www.washingtontimes.com/news/2016/jul/15/renu-khator-university-of-houston-president-defend/kip.

67. *See* Laura Kipnis, *My Title IX Inquisition*, CHRON. OF HIGHER ED. (May 29, 2015), http://chronicle.com/article/My-Title-IX-Inquisition/230489/.

68. The White House, Remarks: The President's Commencement Address at Rutgers State University (2016), *available at* https://www.whitehouse.gov/the-press-office/2016/05/15/remarks-president-commencement-address-rutgers-state-university-new.

69. Robert M. O'Neil, FREE SPEECH IN THE COLLEGE COMMUNITY 22 (1997).

70. There are many accounts of FSM, but for an overview, see Jo Freeman, *The Berkeley Free Speech Movement, in* ENCYC. OF AM. SOC. MOVEMENTS 1178–82 (Immanuel Ness, ed., 2004). The details that follow were taken from this source. The archives, including amazing photographs of the unfolding events, can be found at University of California, Calisphere: The Free Speech Movement (2005), *available at* https://calisphere.org/exhibitions/43/the-free-speech-movement/.

71. Jeffery Kahn, *Ronald Reagan Launched Political Career Using the Berkeley Campus as a Target*, UC BERKELEY NEWS (June 8, 2004), http://www.berkeley.edu/news/media/releases/2004/06/08_reagan.shtml.

72. For a related discussion, see Rodney Smolla, *Academic Freedom, Hate Speech, and the Idea of a University*, 53 LAW AND CONTEMP. PROBLEMS 195, 216–17 (1990).

73. *See* Jodi S. Cohen, *University of Illinois Oks $875,000 Settlement to End Steven Salaita Dispute*, CHI. TRIB. (Nov. 12, 2015), http://www.chicagotribune.com/news/local/breaking/ct-steven-salaita-settlement-met-20151112-story.html.

74. *"Stupid and Offensive,"* UO MATTERS (Nov. 2, 2016), http://uomatters.com/2016/11/stupid-and-offensive.html.

75. *See Student Quits at UCLA over Rant,* N.Y. Times (March 19, 2011), http://www.nytimes.com/2011/03/20/us/20rant.html. UCLA correctly refused to discipline the student but she nevertheless withdrew, reportedly because of ongoing harassment and ostracization.

76. American Association of University Professors, *Reports and Publications: 1940 Statement of Principles on Academic Freedom and Tenure* (2015), *available at* https://www.aaup.org/report/1940-statement-principles-academic-freedom-and-tenure.

77. *Id.*

78. *Id.*

79. 385 U.S. 589, 603 (1967). *See also* Marjorie Heins, Priests of Our Democracy: The Supreme Court, Academic Freedom, and the Anti-Communist Purge (2013).

80. Ronald Dworkin, *We Need a New Interpretation of Academic Freedom, in* The Future of Academic Freedom, at 189–90.

CHAPTER 4. HATE SPEECH

1. *See, e.g.,* Charles R. Lawrence, III, *If He Hollers Let Him Go: Regulating Racist Speech on Campus,* 1990 Duke L.J. 431; Mari Matsuda, *Public Response to Racist Speech: Considering the Victim's Story,* 87 Mich. L. Rev. 2320 (1989); David Kretzmer, *Freedom of Speech and Racism,* 8 Cardozo L. Rev. 445 (1987); Richard Delgado, *Words That Wound: A Tort Action for Racial Insults, Epithets, and Name-Calling,* 17 Harv. C.R.-C.L.L. Rev. 133 (1982) (all favoring restrictions on hate speech).

2. PEN America, *And Campus for All: Diversity, Inclusion and Freedom of Speech at U.S. Universities* 10 (2016) (describing a dozen speech codes being declared unconstitutional). *See, e.g., Dambrot v. Central Mich. Univ.,* 55 F.3d 1177, 1185 (6th Cir. 1995) (First Amendment challenge to Central Michigan University's "discriminatory harassment policy"); *UWM Post, Inc. v. Bd. of Regents of the Univ. of Wis. System,* 774 F. Supp. 1163 (E.D. Wis. 1991) (challenging the University of Wisconsin's hate speech code); *Doe v. Univ. of Mich.,* 721 F. Supp. 852, 867 (E.D. Mich. 1989) (challenge to University of Michigan hate speech code).

3. Jeremy Waldron, The Harm in Hate Speech 8–9 (2012).

4. *Id.* at 8.

5. Richard Delgado, *Words that Wound: A Tort Action for Racial Insults, Epithets, and Name Calling, in* WORDS THAT WOUND 94 (Mari Matsuda et al., eds.) (1993).

6. Mari J. Matsuda, *Public Response to Racist Speech: Considering the Victim's Story, in* WORDS THAT WOUND, at 24.

7. Waldron, THE HARM IN HATE SPEECH, at 4.

8. *Id.* at 85.

9. *Id.*

10. *Id.* at 5.

11. Delgado, *Words that Wound*, at 94.

12. Charles R. Lawrence III, *If He Hollers Let Him Go: Regulating Racist Speech on Campus, in* WORDS THAT WOUND, at 62.

13. Catharine MacKinnon, ONLY WORDS 73 (1993).

14. *Id.* at 67–68.

15. *Id.* at 69.

16. Timothy C. Shiell, HATE SPEECH ON TRIAL 31 (2d ed. 2009).

17. Matsuda, *Public Response to Racist Speech*, at 30.

18. 343 U.S. 250 (1952).

19. *Id.* at 251.

20. *Id.* at 258.

21. *Id.* at 266.

22. Indeed, the United States Court of Appeals for the Seventh Circuit has expressly said that it does not believe that *Beauharnais* survives and is any longer good law. *See Am. Booksellers Assn. v. Hudnut*, 771 F.2d 323 (9th Cir. 1985); *Collin v. Smith*, 578 F.2d 1197, 1204–5 (7th Cir. 1978).

23. *See* 376 U.S. 254 (1964).

24. Jeremy Waldron, who advocates regulation of hate speech, acknowledges that "Joseph Beauharnais's conviction would not be upheld today." Waldron, THE HARM IN HATE SPEECH, at 64.

25. R.A.V. v. City of St. Paul, 505 U.S. 377 (1992). *See also Dawson v. Delaware*, 503 U.S. 159 (1992) (holding that it was reversible error for a jury to be instructed that a defendant was a member of the Aryan Brotherhood, which was stipulated to be a "white racist gang," because it was irrelevant and violated the First Amendment).

26. *Nationalist Socialist Party of Am. v. Village of Skokie*, 432 U.S. 43, 44 (1977).

27. 69 Ill. 2d 605, 373 N.E.2d 21 (1978).

28. *Collin,* 578 F.2d at 1197. The Supreme Court denied a stay of this decision. *Smith v. Collin,* 436 U.S. 953 (1978).

29. *See* Lawrence, *If He Hollers Let Him Go,* at 66–71.

30. 315 U.S. 568 (1942).

31. *Id.* at 569.

32. *Id.* at 571–72 (emphasis added).

33. *Id.* at 571 (citation omitted).

34. *See* Kent Greenawalt, *Insults and Epithets: Are They Protected Speech?* 42 RUTGERS L. REV. 287 (1990).

35. 403 U.S. 15 (1971).

36. *Id.* at 20.

37. 491 U.S. 397 (1989).

38. *Id.* at 409.

39. 405 U.S. 518 (1972).

40. *Id.* at 529 (Burger, C.J., dissenting).

41. 408 U.S. 901 (1972).

42. *Id.* at 913.

43. *Id.* at 914.

44. 505 U.S. 377 (1992).

45. *Id.* at 380.

46. *Id.* at 386 (citations omitted).

47. *Id.* at 391.

48. For example, in *Virginia v. Black,* 538 U.S. 343, 359 (2003), the Court declared: "A state may punish those words 'which by their very utterance inflict injury or tend to incite an immediate breach of the peace.' We have consequently held that fighting words . . . are generally proscribable under the First Amendment."

49. *Id.* at 343.

50. *Id.* at 359–60.

51. 508 U.S. 476 (1993).

52. *Id.* at 487–88.

53. A recent report by PEN America notes that "Over the past two decades, courts have overturned speech codes at a dozen colleges and universities." PEN America, *And Campus for All: Diversity, Inclusion amd Freedom of Speech at U.S. Universities* 10 (2016). *See, e.g., Dambrot,* 55 F.3d

at 1185; *UWM Post*, 774 F. Supp. 1163 (Wisconsin's hate speech code); *Doe v. Univ. of Mich.*, 721 F. Supp. 852, 867 (E.D. Mich. 1989).

54. These facts are found in *Doe v. Univ. of Mich.*, 721 F. Supp. at 856.

55. *Id.*

56. *Id.* at 858.

57. Kent Greenawalt, FIGHTING WORDS 76–77 (1995).

58. *Id.* at 76; 721 F.Supp. at 861.

59. 721 F.Supp. at 861.

60. *See id.*

61. *Id.* at 867.

62. *UWM Post*, 774 F. Supp. 1163.

63. *Id.* at 1166.

64. *IOTA XI Ch. of Sigma Chi Fraternity v. Geo. Mason Univ.*, 993 F.2d 386, 393 (4th Cir. 1993).

65. *Corry v. Leland Stan. Junior Univ.*, No. 704309 (Super. Ct. of Santa Clara Cty., Feb. 27, 1995).

66. *Id.*

67. CAL. EDUC. CODE, §367(a).

68. *Corry v. Stan. Univ.*, at 42.

69. *See* Shiell, HATE SPEECH ON TRIAL, at 4.

70. Lawrence, *If He Hollers Let Him Go*, at 67. The Stanford Code, too, was invalidated when challenged. *See Corry v. Stan. Univ.*

71. Waldron, THE HARM IN HATE SPEECH, at 8–9.

72. *Grutter v. Bollinger*, 509 U.S. 306, 373 (2003) (Thomas, J., dissenting).

73. Nadine Strossen, *Regulating Racist Speech on Campus: A Modest Proposal*, 1990 DUKE L.J. 484, 556.

74. *See id.* at 557.

75. Henry Louis Gates Jr. et al., SPEAKING OF RACE, SPEAKING OF SEX: HATE SPEECH, CIVIL RIGHTS, AND CIVIL LIBERTIES 45 (1994).

76. Vejdeland and Others v. Sweden, App. No. 1813/07, Eur. Ct. H.R., Judgment, ¶15 (Feb. 9, 2012), http://hudoc.echr.coe.int/eng#{"itemid":["001–109046"]}.

77. Féret v. Belgium, App. No. 15615/07, Eur. Ct. H.R., Judgment, ¶41 (July 16, 2009), http://hudoc.echr.coe.int/eng#{"itemid":["001–93626"]}.

78. Vejdeland, at ¶60; Féret, at ¶82.

79. *See* Vanessa Gera, *Polish Court Fines Catholic Magazine for Comparing Woman Who Sought Abortion to Nazis*, Canadian Press (Sept. 23, 2009).

80. *See Bardot Fined Over Racial Hatred*, BBC News: Entm't (June 3, 2008), http://news.bbc.co.uk/2/hi/entertainment/7434193.stm.

81. *See Internet Bigot Stephen Birrell Jailed for Eight Months*, BBC News (Oct. 17, 2011), http://www.bbc.com/news/uk-scotland-glasgow-west–15333744.

82. *See* John Onyando, *Kenya: Dubious Uses of Hate Speech Laws*, All Africa (Oct. 17, 2015), http://allafrica.com/stories/201510190792.html.

83. *See* Nina Siegal, *Geert Wilders, Dutch Politician, Distracts from Hate-Speech Trial with More Vitriol*, N.Y. Times (Oct. 31, 2016), http://www.nytimes.com/2016/11/01/world/europe/geert-wilders-netherlands-hate-trial.html, and Max Bearak, *"Prosecuted for What Millions Think": Netherlands Hate Speech Trial Restarts for Geert Wilders*, Wash. Post (Oct. 14, 2016), https://www.washingtonpost.com/news/worldviews/wp/2016/10/14/prosecuted-for-what-millions-think-geert-wilderss-hate-speech-trial-gets-green-light/.

84. Strossen, *Regulating Racist Speech on Campus*, at 561.

85. *See* Jacob Mchangama, *The Harm in Hate Speech Laws*, Policy Review (Dec. 1, 2012), http://www.hoover.org/research/harm-hate-speech-laws; see also *Changing Attitudes on Gay Marriage*, Pew Research Center (May 12, 2016), http://www.pewforum.org/2016/05/12/changing-attitudes-on-gay-marriage/, Mike Brunker, Monica Alba, and Bill Dedman, *Hate Crime in America, by the Numbers*, Nbcnews.com (June 18, 2015), http://www.nbcnews.com/storyline/charleston-church-shooting/hate-crime-america-numbers-n81521, *The Global Divide on Homosexuality*, Pew Research Center (June 4, 2013), http://www.pewglobal.org/2013/06/04/the-global-divide-on-homosexuality/, and James Kirchick, *If You Want to Combat Hate, Don't Outlaw Hate Speech–Counter It with Better Ideas*, Tablet (Feb. 12, 2014), http://www.tabletmag.com/jewish-news-and-politics/162657/free-hate-speech.

86. *Cohen v. Cal.*, 403 U.S. 15, 26 (1971).

CHAPTER 5. WHAT CAMPUSES CAN AND CAN'T DO

1. We recognize, of course, that there could be categories of what can't be done under current law, but should be allowed (or what can be done, but shouldn't be allowed). We do not identify any such areas, so our discussion of "can" and "should" is the same, as is "can't" and "shouldn't."

2. 394 U.S. 576, 592 (1969).

3. 438 U.S. 726, 745–46 (1978).

4. 491 U.S. 397, 414 (1989).

5. 485 U.S. 312, 322 (1988).

6. 562 U.S. 443 (2011).

7. *Id.* at 448.

8. *Id.* at 458 (citation omitted).

9. Editorial Board, *Straightjacketed at the University of Oregon: Editorial*, OREGONIAN (Nov. 10, 2016), http://www.oregonlive.com/opinion/index.ssf/2016/11/straight-jacketed_at_the_unive.html, Ofer Raban, *A Teachable Moment on Practicing What We Preach*, OREGONIAN (Nov. 14, 2016), http://www.oregonlive.com/opinion/index.ssf/2016/11/a_teachable_moment_on_practici.html#incart_opinion, *"Stupid and Offensive,"* UO MATTERS (Nov. 2, 2016), http://uomatters.com/2016/11/stupid-and-offensive.html, and *University of Oregon Investigative Report* (Nov. 20, 2016), https://provost.uoregon.edu/sites/provost1.uoregon.edu/files/final_investigative_report_redacted_-_final.pdf.

10. We disagree with University of Illinois College of Law dean Vikram Amar, who argued that the professor's actions "may undermine her . . . trust and credibility with students, alumni and the community." Vikram Amar, *First Monday Musings: On Academic Freedom, Administrative Fairness, and Blackface*, ABOVE THE LAW (Nov. 7, 2016), http://abovethelaw.com/2016/11/first-monday-musings-on-academic-freedom-administrative-fairness-and-blackface/. If that is enough to justify suspending or removing a professor, it would provide a basis for doing so any time a faculty member participates in activities that make a significant number of students uncomfortable. The speech of faculty members would be greatly restricted if it could be punished whenever it risks offending some of the students. *See also* Eugene Volokh, *At the University of Oregon, No More Free Speech for Professors on Subjects such as Race, Religion, Sexual Orientation*, WASH. POST (Dec. 26, 2016), https://

www.washingtonpost.com/news/volokh-conspiracy/wp/2016/12/26/
at-the-university-of-oregon-no-more-free-speech-for-professors-
on-subjects-such-as-race-religion-sexual-orientation/?utm_term=.
64adb456c7fo.

11. The Supreme Court also has said that fighting words are a category of unprotected speech. *Chaplinsky v. New Hampshire*, 315 U.S. 568
(1942). But as explained in Chapter 4, no fighting words conviction has
been upheld since 1942 and subsequent cases make drafting a constitutional law prohibiting fighting words very unlikely.

12. Incitement of illegal activity also may be a basis for punishing
speech on campuses, though it has not been the focus of the recent efforts to punish speech. The Court has struggled with a definition of
when speech constitutes incitement that can be punished. The current
standard for when speech can be punished as incitement is found in
Brandenburg v. Ohio, 394 U.S. 444, 447 (1969), where the Court said:
"The constitutional guarantees of free speech and free press do not permit a State to forbid or proscribe advocacy of the use of force or of
law violation except where such advocacy is directed to inciting or producing imminent lawless action and is likely to incite or produce such
action." A conviction for incitement under *Brandenburg* only is constitutional if several requirements are met: imminent harm, a likelihood of
producing illegal action, and an intent to cause imminent illegality.

13. *Id.* at 705.

14. *Id.* at 707.

15. *Id.* at 708.

16. *Virginia v. Black*, 538 U.S. 343, 359–60 (2003).

17. *Id.* at 360.

18. *Planned Parenthood of Columbia/Willamette, Inc. v. Am. Coal. of
Life Activists*, 290 F.3d 1058 (9th Cir. 2002).

19. *Id.*

20. Catharine MacKinnon, SEXUAL HARASSMENT OF WORKING
WOMEN 127 (1979).

21. *See, e.g.*, Eugene Volokh, *Freedom of Speech and Workplace Harassment*, 39 UCLA L. Rev. 1791 (1992); Kingsley R. Browne, *Title VII as
Censorship: Hostile-Environment Harassment and the First Amendment*,
52 OHIO ST. L.J. 481 (1991); Marcy Strauss, *Sexist Speech in the Workplace*, 25 HARV. C.R.-C.L. L. REV. 1 (1990) (all describing the First

Amendment issues involved in regulating speech that creates a hostile environment). *See also Robinson v. Jacksonville Shipyards, Inc.,* 760 F. Supp. 1486 (D. Fla. 1991) (finding liability for sexual harassment based largely on the persuasive presence of pornography creating a hostile and intimidating environment).

22. *Meritor Savings Bank v. Vinson,* 477 U.S. 57, 66–67 (1986).

23. 29 C.F.R. §1604.11 (1998).

24. It provides: "No person in the United States shall, on the basis of sex, be excluded from participation in, be denied the benefits of, or be subjected to discrimination under any education program or activity receiving federal financial assistance."

25. *See, e.g., Sexual Harassment Guidance: Harassment of Students by School Employees, Other Students, or Third Parties,* 62 FED. REG. 12034 (1997) (recognizing sexual harassment, including the creation of a hostile environment, as a form of sex discrimination under Title IX of the Education Amendments of 1972); *Racial Incidents and Harassment Against Students at Educational Institutions: Investigative Guidance,* 59 FED. REG. 11448 (1994) (providing similar guidance on racial harassment as a form of race discrimination under Title VI of the Civil Rights Act of 1964).

26. 503 U.S. 60 (1991).

27. *Spotlight: Correcting Common Mistakes in Campus Speech Policies,* FOUND. FOR INDIVIDUAL RIGHTS IN EDUC., available at https://www.thefire.org/spotlight/correcting-common-mistakes-in-campus-speech-policies/.

28. Cara McClellan, *Discrimination as Disruption: Addressing Hostile Environments Without Violating the Constitution,* 34 YALE L. & POL'Y REV. INTER ALIA 1, 3 (2015).

29. *Id.* at 3.

30. *See, e.g.,* Mary Bowerman, *University of Pennsylvania Investigating Racist "Lynching" Group Thread,* USA TODAY (Nov. 11, 2016), http://www.usatoday.com/story/news/nation-now/2016/11/11/university-pennsylvania-investigating-racially-charged-group-thread/93669194/ (describing an incident at the University of Pennsylvania where this occurred and African American students were sent a text message with a racially charged message and threats of lynching).

31. Geoffrey Stone, *Statement on Principles of Free Inquiry,* UCHICAGONEWS: BEHIND THE NEWS (July 2012), available at https://news.

uchicago.edu/behind-the-news/free-expression/statement-principles-free-inquiry.

32. 452 U.S. 640, 648 (1981).

33. *Id.*

34. *Id.* at 654.

35. 336 U.S. 77 (1949).

36. 408 U.S. 104, 107–8 (1972).

37. *Id.* at 116.

38. *ADF Lawsuit Results in Speech Policy Changes at Phoenix Community Colleges*, ARIZONA DAILY INDEPENDENT (Nov. 8, 2016), https://arizonadailyindependent.com/2016/11/08/adf-lawsuit-results-in-speech-policy-changes-at-phoenix-community-colleges/.

39. 487 U.S. 474 (1988).

40. *Id.* at 487.

41. 307 U.S. 496 (1939).

42. 308 U.S. 147 (1939).

43. 307 U.S. at 515 (Roberts, J., concurring).

44. 308 U.S. at 162.

45. *See also Jamison v. Texas*, 318 U.S. 413 (1943) (declaring unconstitutional a city's ordinance that prohibited the distribution of leaflets and expressly rejecting the city's argument of an absolute right to control speech on public property).

46. *Id.* at 163.

47. 354 U.S. 234 (1957).

48. *Id.* at 250.

49. 547 U.S. 410 (2006).

50. *See, e.g., Pickering v. Board of Educ.*, 391 U.S. 563 (1968) (government employee's speech is protected by the First Amendment if it involves a matter of public concern and does not unduly interfere with the functioning of the workplace).

51. 547 U.S. at 421.

52. *Id.* at 438 (Souter, J., dissenting) ("I have to hope that today's majority does not mean to imperil First Amendment protection of academic freedom in public colleges and universities, whose teachers necessarily speak and write 'pursuant to . . . official duties.' ").

53. *Id.* at 425.

54. *Demers v. Austin*, 746 F.3d 402, 412 (9th Cir. 2014).

55. For an overview and discussion of these developments see Robert C. Post, *Academic Freedom and the "Intifada Curriculum"* (2003) FACULTY SCHOLARSHIP SERIES, available at http://digitalcommons.law.yale.edu/fss_papers/183.

56. *Id.*

57. *Id.*

58. *Id.*

59. *See* Kim D. Chanbonpin, *Crisis and Trigger Warnings: Reflections on Legal Education and the Social Value of the Law*, 90 CHI.-KENT L. REV. 615, 623 (2015).

60. *Id.* at 624.

61. *Id.* at 623.

62. *See FCC v. Pacifica Found.*, 438 U.S. 726 (1978).

63. Chanbonpin writes: "Making trigger warnings available on course materials is one way for students to reclaim power. The student-led call for their use creates an opportunity for faculty to thoughtfully curate the classroom as a democratic space 'where students gain a public voice and come to grips with their own power as individuals and social agents.' With content advisories, students can decide for themselves whether to attend class or how to participate in classroom discussion." Chanbonpin, *Crisis and Trigger Warnings*, at 632.

64. *See, e.g.*, Greg Lukianoff and Jonathan Haidt, *The Coddling of the American Mind*, ATLANTIC (Sept. 2015).

65. *See* Erica Goldberg, *Free Speech Consequentialism*, 116 COLUM. L. REV. 687, 750 (2016) (trigger warnings have a chilling effect on course material and professorial free speech).

66. American Association of University Professors, *On Trigger Warnings* (2014), https://www.aaup.org/report/trigger-warnings.

67. Emily Crockett, *Safe Spaces, Explained*, VOX.COM (Aug. 25, 2016), http://www.vox.com/2016/7/5/11949258/safe-spaces-explained, and Sarah Brown and Katherine Mangan, *What "Safe Spaces" Really Look Like on College Campuses*, CHRON. OF HIGHER ED. (Sept. 8, 2016), http://www.chronicle.com/article/What-Safe-Spaces-Really/237720.

68. Rachael Pells, *NUS "No Platform" Policy Goes "Too Far" and Threatens Free Speech, Peter Tatchell Warns*, THE INDEP. (April 25, 2016), http://www.independent.co.uk/news/uk/nus-no-platform-safe-space-policy-goes-too-far-threatens-free-speech-warns-peter-tatchell-

a6999801.html (claim by students that universities should "balance freedom of speech and freedom from harm" in order to accommodate "safer space activism").

69. Nina Burleigh, *The Battle Against "Hate Speech" on College Campuses Gives Rise to a Generation that Hates Speech,* NEWSWEEK (May 26, 2016), http://www.newsweek.com/2016/06/03/college-campus-free-speech-thought-police–463536.html.

70. Katherine Timpf, *Students and Faculty Petition to Defund Campus Newspaper Because It's Not a "Safe Space,"* NATIONAL REVIEW (Sept. 22, 2015), http://www.nationalreview.com/article/424473/students-and-faculty-petition-defund-campus-newspaper-because-its-not-safe-space.

71. Dana Kampa, *Conservative Pundit Ben Shapiro Lectures to Turbulent Crowd on Safe Spaces, Freedom of Speech,* BADGER HERALD (Nov. 17, 2016), https://badgerherald.com/news/2016/11/17/conservative-pundit-ben-shapiro-lectures-to-turbulent-crowd-on-safe-spaces-freedom-of-speech/.

72. Heben Nigatu, *21 Racial Microaggressions that You Hear on a Daily Basis,* BUZZFEED (Dec. 3, 2013) https://www.buzzfeed.com/hnigatu/racial-microaggressions-you-hear-on-a-daily-basis?utm_term=.bi2n3bKvx9#.svrwezpEVy.

73. 551 U.S. 661 (2010).

74. *Id.* at 670–71.

75. *Id.* at 686–87.

76. *Id.* at 688.

77. *See, e.g.,* Hallye Bankson, *Maintaining the Schoolhouse Gate: Why Public Universities Should Not Regulate Online, Off Campus Communications Through Student Handbooks,* 43 J.L. & EDUC. 127 (2014).

78. Jeffrey C. Sun, Neil H. Hutchens, and James D. Breslin, *A Virtual Land of Confusion with College Students' Online Speech: Introducing the Curricular Nexus Test,* 16 U. PA. J. CNST. L. 49, 52 (2013).

79. *See* Elissa Kerr, *Professional Standards on Social Media: How Colleges and Universities Have Denied Students' Constitutional Rights and Courts Refused to Intervene,* 41 J.C. & U.L. 601, 618 (2015).

80. 816 N.W.2d 509 (Minn. 2012).

81. *Id.* at 512.

82. *Id.*

83. *Id.*

84. *See Davis v. Monroe Cty.,* 526 U.S. 629 (1999).

85. It is important to stress that the Supreme Court also has said that "Deliberate indifference makes sense as a theory of direct liability ... only where the funding recipient has some control over the alleged harassment. A recipient cannot be directly liable for its indifference where it lacks the authority to take remedial action." *Id.* at 646.

86. *Whitney v. Cal.*, 274 U.S. 357, 375, 377 (1927) (Brandeis, J., concurring).

87. Stone, *Statement on Principles of Free Inquiry.*

88. Michael E. Miller, *Swastika at Bowie State as Threats, Resignations, Protests Spread Across American Colleges*, WASH. POST: MORNING MIX (Nov. 13, 2015), https://www.washingtonpost.com/news/morning-mix/wp/2015/11/13/swastika-at-bowie-state-as-threats-resignations-protests-spread-across-american-colleges/.

89. Deb Belt, *Swastika Denounced By Bowie State Students, Staff*, BOWIE PATCH (Nov. 23, 2015), http://patch.com/maryland/bowie/swastika-denounced-bowie-state-students-staff-0.

90. Tim Cohn, *Faculty Pen Letter to Schlissel About Diag Chalking Incident*, MICH. DAILY (APR. 17, 2016), https://www.michigandaily.com/section/news/480-faculty-members-pen-letter-pres-schlissel-about-diag-chalking-incidents.

91. *Id.*

92. Message from Vice Chancellor Parham, available at http://studentaffairs.uci.edu/VC_free_speech.php.

93. *Kalven Committee: Report on the University's Role in Political and Social Action* (Nov. 11, 1967), http://www-news.uchicago.edu/releases/07/pdf/kalverpt.pdf.

CHAPTER 6. WHAT'S AT STAKE?

1. *See* Jelani Cobb, *Race and the Free Speech Diversion*, NEW YORKER (Nov. 10, 2015), http://www.newyorker.com/news/news-desk/race-and-the-free-speech-diversion; Conor Friedersdorf, *Free Speech Is No Diversion*, ATLANTIC (Nov. 12, 2015), http://www.theatlantic.com/politics/archive/2015/11/race-and-the-anti-free-speech-diversion/415254/.

2. Cobb, *Race and the Free Speech Diversion.*

3. Danny Funt, *At Yale, a Fiery Debate over Who's Being Silenced*, COLUM. JOURNALISM REV. (Dec. 22, 2015), http://www.cjr.org/the_feature/yale_free_speech_campus_news.php.

4. See Andrew McGill, *The Missing Black Students at Elite American Universities*, ATLANTIC (Nov. 23, 2015), http://www.theatlantic.com/politics/archive/2015/11/black-college-student-body/417189/; Meredith Kolodner, *Black Students Are Drastically Underrepresented at Top Public Colleges, Data Show*, HECHINGER REPORT (Dec. 18, 2015), http://hechingerreport.org/black-students-are-drastically-underrepresented-at-top-public-colleges-data-show/; Noliwe M. Rooks, *The Biggest Barrier to Elite Education Isn't Affordability. It's Accessibility*, TIME (Feb. 27, 2013), http://ideas.time.com/2013/02/27/the-biggest-barrier-to-elite-education-isnt-affordability-its-accessibility/.

5. Gallup, Knight Found., and Newseum Inst., *Free Expression on Campus: A Survey of U.S. College Students and U.S. Adults*, GALLUP, http://www.knightfoundation.org/media/uploads/publication_pdfs/FreeSpeech_campus.pdf.

6. Eugene Volokh, *No, There's No "Hate Speech" Exception to the First Amendment*, WASH. POST: VOLOKH CONSIPRACY (May 7, 2015), https://www.washingtonpost.com/news/volokh-conspiracy/wp/2015/05/07/no-theres-no-hate-speech-exception-to-the-first-amendment/?utm_term=.369ad7817eb4.

7. *Report of the Committee on Freedom of Expression at Yale*, YALE COLL. (Dec. 23, 1974), http://yalecollege.yale.edu/deans-office/policies-reports/report-committee-freedom-expression-yale.

8. See Robert Reinhold, *Shockley Debates Montagu as Innis Angrily Pulls Out*, N.Y. TIMES (Dec. 5, 1973), http://www.nytimes.com/1973/12/05/archives/shockley-debates-montagu-as-innis-angrily-pulls-out-tests-called.html; Joel N. Shurkin, BROKEN GENIUS: THE RISE AND FALL OF WILLIAM SHOCKLEY, CREATOR OF THE ELECTRONIC AGE (2006).

9. *Shockley and Innis Are Again Denied Forum for Debate*, N.Y. TIMES (Feb. 18, 1974), http://www.nytimes.com/1974/02/18/archives/shockley-and-innis-are-again-denied-forum-for-debate.html?_r=0.

10. *Report of the Committee on Freedom of Expression at Yale*.

11. Diana C. Mutz, HEARING THE OTHER SIDE: DELIBERATIVE VERSUS PARTICIPATORY DEMOCRACY (2006). *See also* Amy Gutmann and Dennis Thompson, WHY DELIBERATIVE DEMOCRACY? (2004).

Acknowledgments

This book grew out of our experience teaching a freshman undergraduate seminar, "Free Speech on College Campuses," at the University of California, Irvine, in the Winter 2016 quarter. It was a wonderful teaching experience as we had fifteen superb students who were constantly willing to engage with the material and discuss difficult issues. But teaching this course also caused us to realize that this generation of college students is different in its understanding and commitment to freedom of speech and in its laudable desire to make sure that campuses are protective and inclusive of all students.

We wrote some essays on our experience teaching the class and the lessons we learned from it. We were thrilled when Bill Frucht, at Yale University Press, suggested our writing a book on the topic. Bill has been terrific, helping us to shape the thesis of the book, providing us a great edit, and constantly encouraging us. We are grateful to our literary agent, Bonnie Nadell, who handled all of the details for us.

ACKNOWLEDGMENTS

We want to thank our research assistants, Alina Ananian, Kevin Barnes, and Laura Lively, for their excellent assistance. We also are very appreciative of our colleagues at the University of California, Irvine, School of Law for their insightful comments and suggestions on an earlier draft of the manuscript.

We dedicate this book to our students who constantly challenge us, impress us, and inspire us. Teaching them remains the very best part of our wonderful professional lives.

Index

abolitionism, 33
abortion, 33–34, 117, 129
Abrams, Jacob, 38
Abrams v. United States (1919), 38
academic freedom, 7, 21, 60, 155;
    benefits of, 62; as core value, x–xi,
    67, 80–81, 112, 132; professionalism
    linked to, 53, 65–66, 68, 69, 76,
    78–79, 134–35; in public vs. private
    institutions, 53, 113; threats to,
    69–70, 137, 154
Adams, Charles, 170 n. 22
Adams, John, 32
affirmative action, 106, 138, 154
Alexander VI, Pope, 28
Alien and Sedition Acts (1798), 32
Alito, Samuel, 115
Alpha Phi, 5
Amar, Vikram, 181–82 n. 10
American Anti-Slavery Society, 33
American Association of University
    Professors (AAUP), 59–61, 62, 65,
    76, 78–79, 137
American Civil Liberties Union, 37
American Psychological Association,
    64
Amherst College, 55
anarchism, 35, 58
Anti-Defamation League, 109

anti-Semitism, 15, 85, 106, 109
anti-slavery movement, 33
antiwar movement, 11, 13, 40, 62,
    76, 93
Areopagitica (Milton), 29–30
Aristophanes, 34
Aristotle, 50
Association of American
    Universities, 61–62
Athenian democracy, 28
Atkinson, Richard, 135

Baez, Joan, 75
Balzac, Honoré de, 34
Bardot, Brigitte, 107
Barnett, George "Trey," 1–2
Barrett, Susan, 1–2
Beauharnais v. Illinois (1952), 87–89,
    90
Belgium, 107
Bell Curve, The (Herrnstein and
    Murray), 63–64
Birrell, Stephen, 107–8
Black, Hugo, 42–43
blacklisting, 71
Black Lives Matter movement, 139
Black Man in a White Coat (Tweedy),
    121
Blackstone, William, 31